Miami Vegan

Plant-Based Recipes from the Tropics to Your Table

Ellen Kanner

author of *Feeding the Hungry Ghost: Life, Faith and What to Eat for Dinner*

LCIX Editions, Mt. Pleasant SC

Advance Praise for Miami Vegan

"Ellen Kanner invites you to explore the lush, plant-based treasures of Miami with *Miami Vegan: Plant-Based Recipes: From the Tropics to Your Table.* Embrace the magic of Miami's tropical bounty, with recipes that celebrate fresh, sustainable ingredients and bold flavors from one of the world's most dynamic culinary cities. Perfect for both seasoned vegans and newcomers to plant-based cooking, this collection is a joyous journey through food that nourishes body and soul, all while capturing the unique taste of Miami."
—Nina Curtis, MBA | Director and Executive Chef, Plant'ish & Co. Culinary Arts

"Miami's wildly rich melting pot of cultures and bountiful tropical fruits and vegetables mean one thing—great food. Ellen Kanner takes it a delicious step further, coming up with Miami-flavored recipes that are all plant-based. Classics like Mango Quick Bread and Ripe Sweet Plantains and favorites like Pikliz and Caribbean Curry are among the authentic recipes that celebrate the local foods that make Miami one of the most delicious places on the planet." —Edible South Florida

For Benjamin, devoted recipe taster, lover of pickles and sandwiches, ambitious artistic director, and excellent husband.

You make everything taste better.

Copyright 2025 by Ellen Kanner

All rights reserved
Published by LCIX Editions
Mt Pleasant SC 29464
www.lcixllc.com
ISBN 9781962539210
Library of Congress Control Number 2024952231
Kathleen Ballard Photography credits: cover photo, author photo, p. 64, p. 110, p. 182.

Table of Contents

Introduction—Miami Authentic	vii
Miami Vegan Pantry	ix
305 Insider Intel	xiii
Miami Favorites/Miami Flavors	xiii
Bocaditos—Sips, Snacks, and Small Plates for All-Day (and All-Night) Grazing	**1**
Miami Favorites—Cuban Coffee—Café Cubano	4
Miami Favorites—Dutch Baby	5
Miami Favorites—Vegan Cheese Scones	6
Miami Favorites—Cat Head Biscuits	8
Miami Favorites—Tofu Scramble or Almost Ackee	10
Miami Flavors—French Toast with Caramelized Bananas	12
Miami Flavors—Tropical Granola	14
Miami Flavors—Tropical Porridge	15
Miami Flavors—Summer Blueberry Loaf	17
Miami Favorites—Mango Quick Bread	19
Miami Favorites—Guava Cream Cheese Pastry—Pastelitos de Guayaba	22
Miami Favorites—Caribbean Curried Pumpkin Dip—Pumpkin Talkari	26
Miami Flavors—Pumpkin Bread	28
Miami Favorites—Smoked Sea Dip	29
Miami Favorites—Vegan Pimento Cheese	30
Miami Favorites—Hoecakes	32
Miami Favorites—Cornbread	34
Succulence—Juicy, Fresh, Ripe Tastes of the Tropics	**37**
Miami Favorite—Magic Dust	39
Miami Flavors—Magic Dust Tropical Fruit Plate	40
Miami Flavors—Sheet Pan Panzanella with Charred Summer Vegetables and Cornbread Croutons	42
Miami Flavors—Fireworks Black Bean and Mango Salad	45
Miami Flavors—Green Mango Salad	46
Miami Flavors—Tomato Choka	48
Miami Flavors—Tomato Choka Salad with Chickpea Tofu	49
Miami Flavors—Seven Seed Quinoa with Spinach and Sesame Dressing	52
Miami Flavors—Catalan Spinach	55
Miami Flavors—Miami Beet Salad	56
Miami Flavors—Collard Confetti	57
Miami Flavors—Tropical Slaw	58
Miami Flavors—Miami Vegan Lettuce Cups with Heart	60
Miami Favorites—Papaya-Tofu Ceviche	63
Mushroom Ceviche	65
Hearts of Palm Ceviche with Grapefruit and Avocado	66
Sizzles, Hot Pots, and Potcakes—Miami Mains	**67**
Miami Favorites—Haitian Bean Gravy—Sos Pwa	68
Miami Favorites—Bahamian Chowder	69
Miami Favorites—Djon Djon Rice	73
Miami Flavors—Mushroom Étouffée	75
Miami Favorites—Arroz Con Jaca o Soya—Cuban Rice and Jackfruit or Tempeh	78
Miami Favorites—Picadillo	80
Miami Flavors—Chickpeas with Saffron	81
Miami Favorites—Feijoada	85
Miami Favorites—Cuban Black Beans	88
Miami Flavors—Tacu Tacu	90
Miami Favorites—Caribbean Pigeon Peas and Rice	92
Miami Favorites—Fideuà or Fideos	94

Miami Favorites—Paella	96
Miami Flavors—Angel Hair with Pumpkin, Annatto, and Lime	98
Miami Favorites—Sort of Sancocho	101
Miami Favorites—Collard Tacos with Chile-Charred Onion and Sweet Potato	105
Miami Flavors—Collard Parcels with Chile Pecan Rice	108
Miami Flavors—Caribbean Curry	112
Miami Favorites—Vegan Macaroni and Cheese	115

Extras, Sides, and Salsas — 117

Miami Flavors—Mango Barbecue Sauce	118
Miami Flavors—20-Minute Golden Papaya Chutney	120
Miami Flavors—Nori Dust	121
Miami Favorites—Pikliz	122
Miami Favorites—Chimichurri	123
Miami Flavors—Tamarind Vinaigrette	124
Miami Flavors—Summer Squash Casserole	125
Miami Favorites—Roasted Potatoes—Papas Asada	126
Miami Flavors—Momma's Greens—Sukuma Wiki	128
Miami Flavors—Maque Choux	130
Miami Flavors—Sofkee (Okay, call 'em grits)	132
Miami Flavors—Crispy Grits Cakes	134
Miami Favorites—Two Fish-Free Caviars	136
Miami Flavors—Cowboy Caviar	136
Miami Flavors—Eggplant Caviar	138
Miami Favorites—House-Smoked Tempeh	139
Miami Flavors—Coconut Green Beans	140
Miami Favorites—Ripe Sweet Plantains—Platanos Maduros	143

Azucar! Miami Celebrates Sweetness — 145

Miami Favorites—Iced Cafecito	147
Miami Flavors—Coconut Shortbread	149
Miami Flavors—Magic Mango Mousse	150
Miami Flavors—Sunshine Squares with Chocolate Chunks	152
Miami Flavors—Orange-Scented Almond Cookies	154
Miami Flavors—Triple Gingerbread	156
Miami Favorites—All-Star Upside Down Cake	159
Miami Favorites—Summer Fruit Cobbler	161
Miami Flavors—Strawberry Kuchen	162
Miami Flavors—Strawberry Pudding	163
Miami Flavors—Whipped Coconut Cream	165
Miami Favorites—Chocolate, Orange, and Almond Olive Oil Cake	167
Miami Flavors—Chocolate Orange Glaze	170
Miami Favorites—Rice Pudding—Arroz con Leche	171
Miami Flavors—Latino-Caribbean Sweet Potato Pumpkin Pie—Cazuela in a Crust	173
Miami Flavors—Orange Blossom Tart for Julia Tuttle	175
Miami Favorites—Kinda Key Lime Pie	178

Miami Vegan Menus — 183
Acknowledgments — 186
About the Author — 187
Index — 188

Introduction—Miami Authentic

Potcake. It's the cooked-on crust of beans and rice that sticks at the bottom of the pot. It's also an affectionate island term for mutt. Potcake may lack epicurean approval, but it tastes of all the best bits stuck together. Potcake is how I think of Miami cuisine. Miami is the gateway to the Caribbean and Latin America, a city where Cuba, the Florida Keys, the Yucatan, the West Indies, the Bahamas, Haiti, and South America can all show up on the same plate.

Miami is sweetness, succulence, sunshine, and heat, glittering Biscayne Bay, the sashay of palm trees, the salt tang in the air, and the benevolent sea breeze that keeps things just this side of sweltering (except during hurricane season). It's also epic urban sprawl, downtown Miami gridlock, the South Beach parade of tourists, the tag art and tats of Wynwood, and the city's century-old tendency to remake itself again and again quicker than you can down a cafecito.

"Miami is a lot," as one visiting friend put it. She looked slightly harried. Another snowbird friend gushed, "Miami is *sexy*." Both are true.

Miami can't help but be a little naughty. We're at the ends of the earth, as far south as the United States can take you, with only the Atlantic beyond. For centuries, it's where people have come to outrun the misdeeds they've committed elsewhere.

So what's authentic Miami? What does that taste like? It tastes like potcake. Cuisine, like language, is always evolving. We have access now to ingredients and equipment that didn't exist for our parents and grandparents. I remember helping my grandmother hand-grind the onions and carrots for her cornbread dressing, running them through a device that looked like an instrument of torture. Now I just blitz everything in a food processor. Does that mean it's not legit? Can a recipe for arroz con pollo—a beloved Cuban dish of chicken and rice—get a plant-based makeover with meaty jackfruit and still be legit? It can in Miami. At least it can now. Miami is among the top ten plant-based cities according to *VegNews* and PETA.

Miami was a city of steakhouses when I was a kid. I went vegan anyway. It made me an outlier in my own community, even in my own family. And it made eating a challenge. Forget Beyond Burgers, forget Ben & Jerry's vegan ice cream—they were years away. There were only a handful of plant-based product prototypes, and they were meh. Miami isn't about meh.

To me, Miami is about the technicolor, techniflavor fruits and vegetables of the tropics, and we have those in abundance. As a new vegan, I fell hard for them. It's been a love enduring through the years and through the seasons. We grow food here, lots of it, from the farmland of Homestead and the Redland to the funky urban farms of Wynwood and Little River. Our growing season begins in November, when the rest of the world is feeling the chill, and lasts through May. After that, it's just too hot. But even in the blistering heat of summer, relief is as close as a mango. Anyone who thinks being plantbased is about deprivation clearly hasn't tasted a sweet, sensual, sticky mango plucked fresh from the tree. You might not have a ripe mango within reach, but *Miami Vegan* is designed to let you taste the tropics wherever you are with doable recipes that capture all of Miami's big, bright flavors.

I'm a fifth-generation native. That's like dog years to most Miamians. That makes me an outlier too. I've been a vegan for over 25 years. I've been writing about the intersection of food, wellness, culture, and sustainability for just as long, with my award-winning book *Feeding the Hungry Ghost: Life, Faith and What to Eat for Dinner*, my newsletter Broccoli Rising, and for outlets including *Huffington Post, Civil Eats, Whetstone, Saveur, EatingWell, VegNews, the Miami Herald and Edible South Florida*, which calls me "the entertaining and lovable voice for plant-based food." Entertaining and lovable is good.

Being a native Miamian and longtime vegan sets me apart, but so does another aspect of my nature I can't seem to do anything about. My husband says intensity is my superpower. I care about you, the planet, the animals, fruits, and vegetables in a deep, loving, holistic, soulful way. That's why I'm the soulful vegan. I don't know how marketable that is, but it's what I've got. And that's what makes me the person to take you beyond the palm trees and tourists and bring you *Miami Vegan*.

Getting back to potcake, rice and beans make up a big part of it for this Miami vegan, be it congris, Cuban red beans and rice, Haitian diri ak pwa, hopping john, or Caribbean pigeon peas and rice, livened up with fresh greens from my backyard and sparked with jaunty but off-the-Scoville-scale hot Scotch bonnet pepper. It's all delicious and it's all Miami.

But along with rice, beans, mangoes, and avocados, these days Miami vegan also means award-winning plant-based pastries, over-the-top plant-based parties, pizzas, burgers, and bowls, soul food and soft-serve, made by artisans in Miami's solid, supportive vegan community. We come in many flavors, all of them authentic.

Some of the most ardent plant-based people I know got scared straight—health issues or having the veil of factory farming ripped away. Every reason to eat plants is good, but I do like pleasure, which *Miami Vegan* aims to deliver, whether you live in Miami, Memphis, or Minneapolis. That said, one compelling reason to go vegan is where I live. Miami is perched precariously at sea level on the Atlantic. We're ground zero for rising tides and seem to be hurricanes' favorite target. Climate change is real, and it's happening here now.

Let's talk about Atlantis. It was an ancient island kingdom which may or may not have existed. Plato described it as a great place to live—fertile soil for growing food, lavish architecture for human comfort and beauty, infrastructure that functioned, and city planning that made sense. The problem was the people. Over time, the Atlanteans stopped thinking about the common good, caring only for themselves. So the gods said the hell with Atlantis and sank it.

The way things are going, Miami could be under water by the end of the century. This is my home. And the home of my husband and our new rescue dog—a potcake. I'd rather it didn't go the way of Atlantis. Keeping Miami above water starts with caring about it and caring about your food choices. Numerous studies have shown eating local, seasonal whole foods reduces your environmental impact. When the food is so delectable and so diverse you need never eat the same thing twice, you can treat yourself well and do the world some good too.

Come visit Miami. Wear sunscreen. Eat plants.

Miami Vegan Pantry

I created *Miami Vegan* to be a party on the page. And you're invited. Come in and meet my friends—all the wonderful tropical flavors of Florida and the vegan ingredients that give dishes oomph without animals. Recipes like sancocho (p. 101), a tuber-rich Latin American stew, and Caribbean pigeon peas and rice (p. 93) are Miami-influenced, big-flavored, and designed to satisfy, busting the myth that vegan food leaves you hungry. And they're made with staple ingredients. *Miami Vegan* recipes don't incorporate commercial plant-based meats, but add them if you've a mind to. If fresh tropical produce isn't easily available, frozen works fine. A well-stocked pantry and freezer means you can conjure Miami or at least have the fixings for a meal that makes you smile anytime.

Allspice—Sounds like a spice blend, but it's actually a berry, which grows—where else?—in the Caribbean and South Florida. Dried and ground into powder, it adds a fruity and earthy note to Latin American and Caribbean dishes. Look for it in the spice section of your grocery store.

Annatto—Also called achiote—are the red seeds from the achiote tree. Annatto adds subtle spice and a blush to dishes. Think of annatto powder as the tropics' more affordable version of saffron. If you can't find annatto at your local market, mild, sweet paprika makes a reasonable substitute in these unreasonable days.

Aquafaba—The liquid from a can of chickpeas. Sounds crazy, but it's an amazing plant-based egg equivalent. Even better, this is stuff we've been throwing out for years. Incorporating aquafaba means less waste, more baking wow,

Baking powder—Choose aluminum-free baking powder. It instantly improves the flavor of baked goods and avoids that strange metallic aftertaste you might have experienced. And what do you want with aluminum in your baking powder anyway?

Beans—Black beans, red beans, pigeon peas, chickpeas, lentils—we love a legume. They're the original plant-based protein. They soak up the flavor of whatever they're cooked with, they're pantry-friendly, belly-filling, and affordable.

Cumin—Both whole cumin seeds and ground cumin add a slightly earthy and funky flavor and a subtle low note to many Latin American and Caribbean recipes.

Coconut—Dried, unsweetened coconut flakes, canned full-fat coconut milk, coconut oil, and sweetened condensed coconut milk all feature in *Miami Vegan* recipes, adding pleasing fat and natural sweetness.

Curry—Curry refers to a spice blend that can contain a multitude of warming spices like cumin and coriander plus a little chile heat. Or it's a dish made with these spices. Commercially blended curry powders do the work for you but vary in spiciness. By a lot. Many Caribbean curries get their spice from a mellow Jamaican curry blend, relying on the island's native spices like turmeric and allspice. It's not killer spicy, just gently warming.

Curry is also a small, slow-growing tree belonging to the citrus family. Originally from India, it does well in Miami. Curry leaves add a quiet but haunting note to curries and other dishes. It's often sold frozen in Indian and Asian markets and online.

Evaporated cane sugar—Sugar with a slightly golden color and sandy texture, evaporated cane sugar performs like white sugar in these recipes but is minimally processed and free of white sugar's animal product refining agents. Available in most grocery stores and online.

Extra virgin olive oil—The highest grade olive oil, heart-healthy, high in polyphenols—plant-based antioxidants, with an herbaceous to grassy flavor and a peppery finish. Cold-pressing the olives right after harvest provides maximum flavor and preserves the antioxidants. Yes, you can cook with it. In fact, you should.

Flour—Unless otherwise indicated, the flour of choice throughout is unbleached all-purpose flour. That's regular do-it-all wheat flour minus the bleaching chemical agents.

Hearts of palm—The tender inner core of certain tropical palms that once grew so plentifully in South Florida, folks called it swamp cabbage. It's much gentler in taste and texture than cabbage. It tastes a little salty like celery but without the strings and the snap. Look for canned sustainable or organic hearts of palm.

Hot sauce—Like curry powder, hot sauce can run the gamut, from mild Frank's Red Hot, the favorite for Buffalo sauce, to those with Scotch bonnet, topping out on the chile chart, better known as the Scoville scale. There's one—or a dozen—in your chile heat comfort zone, and a good many made in and around Miami. We grow chiles after all. Local brands include Stanky, Smilin' Island, and Redacted. If you really go for chile heat like I do, look for datil pepper sauce made with fruity, hot datil peppers, unique to north Florida.

Jackfruit—Green, unripe jackfruit can be pulled into strands—like pulled pork but without the cruelty. It has a neutral flavor and can be cooked with every kind of sauce—barbecue, curry, marinara—making it the ideal meat substitute. Ripe and golden, jackfruit turns sweet. Either way, it's nutrient-dense and satisfying for you, sustainable for the planet. And it's big—some growing to St. Bernard-size. That's a lotta jackfruit. It's available at specialty markets and some grocery stores in a more manageable format—deseeded and skinned, canned and brined, or processed in packets.

Liquid smoke—Like it sounds, liquid smoke is smoke condensed to water and bottled. It imparts a smoky richness to dishes without having to light a fire, barbecue anything, or harm a single animal. Find it in many grocery stores, specialty markets, and online.

Nori—Seaweed that's been dried and pressed. You know it as the thin salty wrap for sushi. Nori adds a briny but fish-free flavor of the sea to recipes. Available in Asian and specialty markets and in many grocery stores.

Nutritional yeast—For anyone who says, "I could never give up cheese," meet nutritional yeast, golden, deactivated yeast flakes with a cheesy, umami taste. Affectionately called nooch, it offers more than cheesiness, imparting an elusive rich, savory flavor to dishes. Look for nutritional yeast fortified with B-12 -- one of the few nutrients otherwise unavailable to vegans. Find it in many grocery stores, specialty markets, and online.

Paprika—In Hungary, paprika capital of the world, you can find eight varieties of paprika. Here we get sweet (or plain), hot, and smoked paprika (or pimentón). Plain paprika adds a fruity, earthy flavor to dishes without chile heat. Many *Miami Vegan* recipes call for smoked paprika to impart a little punch and pungency. Recipes calling for paprika indicate plain paprika.

Plant-based milk—Unsweetened oat milk is my go-to in *Miami Vegan* recipes, for baking, and for my morning coffee. Not into oats? Go for a plant-based milk with some natural creaminess and body. Nut milk is fine, but rice milk which tends to be thin and watery, isn't recommended, especially for baking.

Rice—Rice means short grain white rice in most Latin American cookery, and yes, you can use it throughout. That said, for most rice recipes, and unless otherwise noted, I'd love to coax you into trying brown rice. It gets a little whole grain goodness into you, and its slightly nutty flavor has more going on than white rice. Miami is not about meh.

Sea salt—Sea salt is sea water evaporated. It's pure, mineral-rich, minimally processed, and has none of table salt's added caking agents.

Tahini—An age-old ingredient and favorite vegan flavor bomb, tahini (sesame seed paste) adds plush mouthfeel and sesame richness to dishes. Despite its few ingredients—usually just ground sesame seeds—different brands produce different results. Family-owned and women-run Soom is outstanding. You can find it in many supermarkets and online at www.soomfoods.com.

Tamarind—A tropical fruit with a dark sticky pulp, a handful of seeds, and a flavor like molasses meets citrus. Tamarind is used extensively throughout the Caribbean and Latin America. It can go sweet, it can go savory—it's in Worcestershire sauce. Tamarind is available commercially pressed into blocks, as a paste, and as a concentrated syrup.

Tempeh and tofu—Except where noted, *Miami Vegan* recipes call for extra-firm tofu. Preferably, it should bounce. Tofu gets a bad rep for blandness, but neutrality is its strength. It's amazingly versatile. Tempeh, tofu's cousin, is fermented soy shaped into thin, firm nubbly cakes. Fermentation—so good for the microbiome—gives it a mild flavor between earthy and meaty. Most of the soy grown in this country is genetically modified so, when possible, choose organic tempeh and tofu. Both tempeh and tofu are available in most supermarkets and Asian markets.

Vegan butter, cheese, and yogurt—Plant-based progress! Quality commercial vegan dairy products are now widely available in most grocery stores. Look for them sitting alongside their dairy companions in the refrigerated dairy section.

Miami Vegan Produce

Avocado—Football-shaped Florida avocados give you a lot to love. They're bigger than Hass, your guacamole go-tos, with bright green skin and firm, pale yellow flesh. They're lower in fat than Hass and mildly sweet, a reminder that avocados are, botanically speaking, fruit. Split, remove their pit and they're natural bowls. But sure, you can use Hass avocados in these recipes too.

Chile—Judiciously added, fresh chile peppers, be they fire alarm-hot Scotch bonnets or more demure ancho and jalapeños chiles, add dimension to tropical recipes without necessarily flaming you out. If you're sensitive to chile heat, dial them down or leave them out. Avoid chile burn. Wear rubber or latex gloves when chopping chiles. Wash your knife, cutting board, and hands when you're done. Don't make me say it again.

Citrus—Citrus reveals rather than conceals. Lemons, limes, oranges, and grapefruit brighten food without fat. Many *Miami Vegan* recipes call for citrus of one kind or another. When juice is called for, fresh beats bottled by a mile. When possible, juice the citrus just before using. Citrus juice left standing can become more acidic.

Fresh herbs—An easy, instant way to brighten a recipe. A few we use with abandon around here:

- cilantro with its fresh green-meets-citrus flavor
- flat-leaf parsley (cleaner flavor, easier to chop, easier to eat than the curly kind)
- thyme, with its whisper of the Mediterranean
- mint, for natural sweetness

Jicama—Pronounced HIC-ama, it offers excellent crunch and a mild sweet flavor with hints of apple. It's a big brown thing to look at—its other name is Mexican turnip. Some markets like Trader Joe's sell fresh jicama already peeled and sliced into batons for easy eating.

Lemongrass—Lemongrass tastes like its name suggests, a little citrusy, a little grassy. Used in many Thai and Viet dishes, it grows like nobody's business in Miami, including my backyard. Available fresh in many Asian and specialty markets. Lemongrass is also dried and ground as powder, which saves you and your knife from chopping the woody stems. Look for it online.

Mango—The world's favorite fruit has over a thousand different cultivars, and many of them grow in Miami. Mangos are C-rich juicy and make summer in Miami worth the heat and humidity. Choose frozen mango over canned, which tends to be packed in syrup. A good ripe mango offers plenty of natural sweetness and needs no embellishment.

Papaya—According to legend, Columbus called papaya the fruit of angels, and no wonder—it's both food and medicine. Papaya's natural enzymes aid in giving you glowing skin and benefit digestion too. This oblong fruit is firm-fleshed and tastes vegetal when green and unripe, then turns silken and mildly peach-flavored when ripe.

Plantain—A starchy fruit that looks like a big banana. Unripe and green, it's mild-flavored, adding a pleasing body to savory dishes, or crunch when sliced thin and made into chips. Ripe plantain becomes meltingly tender and sweet.

Miami Vegan Product Sourcing

Tropical Produce and Tropical Products

Robert is Here, a Miami institution, located near the entrance to Everglades National Park is your source for fresh tropical produce and locally made chutneys, jams, hot sauces, and more. They ship. https://www.robertishere.com/collections/all

Coconut and Jackfruit Products

Edward and Sons Organic https://store.edwardandsons.com/

For more about tropical produce:
Fairchild Tropical Garden, Miami's award-winning botanical garden www.fairchildgarden.org
Rare Fruit Council https://www.rarefruitcouncil.org/
University of Florida Institute of Food and Agriculture Sciences www.ifas.ufl.edu

Spices

Family-owned Badia has been adding spice to Miami for over 60 years. They're also a source for specialty seeds and spices like annatto powder and paste and canned items like hearts of palm. https://badiaspices.com/

Dried Beans

Camellia www.camelliabrand.com

Heirloom Beans

Rancho Gordo www.ranchogordo.com

Latin American Pantry Staples

Family-owned Conchita, based in Miami, offers Latin American and tropical pantry staples including guava paste, hearts of palm, beans, and rice. www.conchita-foods.com

Established in 1930, Miami-based Iberia is the top food distributor of Latin American and Caribbean spices, condiments, beans, and other pantry staples. www.iberiafoods.com

305 Insider Intel, Miami Flavors, and Miami Favorites

Sprinkled throughout *Miami Vegan* are a few brief sections marked with a palm frond and 305—Miami's main area code. These sections give you a little Miami backstory, a little more local flavor, whether it's about cafecito culture or rice and beans.

Recipes are designated as **Miami Flavors**, those shaped by tropical produce and spices, and **Miami Favorites**, recipes with ties to our culture and community, that give you a taste of who we are. Really, though, they're all favorites.

The few iconic Miami recipes you won't find here are those that can't easily be veganized in a home kitchen. Unless otherwise noted, most *Miami Vegan* recipes are built to last. They can be kept covered and refrigerated for several days.

Bocaditos—Sips, Snacks, and Small Plates for All-Day (and All-Night) Grazing

305 Mealtime in Miami

If you're big on set mealtimes, be prepared. We do things differently in Miami. We eat and drink 24/7 with abandon. There's a reason the beloved Cuban sandwich is called medianoche—midnight. It's a montadito (a bite, a tapas-y sandwich) designed to eat in the middle of the night, when you've just gotten home from a party, too revved to sleep, and are feeling a little peckish. You want your medianoche before lunch? No problema!

Miami loves Sunday brunch, preferably outside at the South Beach or Wynwood hot spot of the minute. We perch and pose and chatter and air kiss, wearing our shades, adult beverage in one hand, cell phone for selfies in the other. We call this experience brunch, but the local crowd is a late one, and we only get rolling in the afternoon. If you go mid-morning, you'll be guaranteed a table almost anywhere. The downside is you'll be eating alone, and the waitstaff may still be slightly party-impaired. They're pretty, but they're young. Be patient.

305 Cafecito Culture

Order a cappuccino after breakfast in Italy, and the locals mutter dark, Italian curses. In Miami, we drink café Cubanos aka cafecitos—it means little coffees—all day and night. There's no wrong time to have a shot. Calle Ocho cafes all have ventanitas—pass-through cafecito windows, with people lining up for their hit of that ambrosial, alchemical sludge of espresso and sugar. Afternoon cafecitos are part of workspace culture in many Miami offices. It's spooned into tiny disposable cups about the size of a NyQuil cap and looks about as glamorous.

Coffee lovers, do not be deceived by the wee thimbleful you're served. Cafecito means little coffee, but this stuff is high-octane, with a one-two punch of espresso and sugar. Cafecito isn't a superfood. But it can feel like it. Beats post-lunch slump.

I introduced a visiting dour Brit colleague to cafecito. One shot and he was hooked. The next day, he showed up with a new look—a big smile, and a canary-colored guayabera—fashion-forward choice, given his English pallor—downing cafecito shots like a Havana native.

How to serve: This is one of the few *Miami Vegan* recipes that benefits by special equipment—a 6-cup moka pot known here as a cafetera, a two-chambered stovetop espresso maker. There's plenty of designer ones, but I have a cheap no-name model that's withstood years of abuse. Most Miami grocery stores stock them, and you can easily find them online. You may be able to make this with an espresso machine, but friends, your fancy Nespresso pod system is not going to help you here.

The coffee, though, is easily sourced in most Miami grocery stores and probably wherever you are. It comes in a brick.

One shot of this stuff is a cafecito. But here's where things get complicated. Add a splash of steamed milk and you've got a cortadito (means small cut). Café con leche—coffee with milk—should really be called leche con café—it's four parts steamed milk to one part espresso, and amazing as it may seem, even more sugar.

    This recipe makes what's called a colada, as in collective. Don't attempt to drink it all yourself. It's meant to be shared. Often you'll see Miami folks pour out shots from a large styrofoam cup. Styrofoam isn't glamorous, isn't eco-friendly, but it's traditional. Change happens slowly. One colada at a time.

Miami Favorites—Cuban Coffee—Café Cubano

How to serve: In shots.

Ingredients

- espresso powder, like Cuban faves Pilon or Cafe Bustelo
- 1/4 cup evaporated cane sugar

Instructions

- Fill the bottom chamber of a 6-cup cafetera, a stovetop moka pot, with water up to the rivet. The amount will vary slightly by maker. Don't worry. Making Cuban coffee is an art, not science. Spoon the espresso powder into the top chamber, leveling it off at the top; then screw the two halves together. Set the pot on the burner over medium-high heat until you hear the whoosh of the water as it forces its way up to where it meets the espresso powder and magically makes espresso.
- Pour sugar into a measuring cup, or perhaps a small cup with a spout for pouring, even a heatproof sippy cup would work. Pour in enough of the brewed espresso—just a few teaspoons—to make very sweet mud.
- Return the cafetera to the burner to complete brewing, then reduce the heat to low to keep the rest of the contents hot.
- Now stir your sugar-espresso sludge. Vigorously. Keep stirring at a good clip until the sugar dissolves and the mixture becomes thick, pale, and cream-like. This is the much desired state known as espumita. There's no such thing as overstirring. This offers time to chat with the barista about the weather, your mother, where to go for a massage, or the best place for hair extensions.
- Once all the espresso has brewed, slowly pour it into the beaker, continuing to stir. When espresso and sugar mud have integrated, pour immediately into espresso cups. If you've done this right, a small pale layer of sugar foam, known as cremita, will rise to the top. This is the crown of your café Cubano. Knock your cafecito back like a local.
- Serves 4 to 6.

Miami Favorites—Dutch Baby

Think of a Dutch baby as the love child of a frittata and a pancake. There's no baby involved and in this vegan version, no eggs either. Extra-firm tofu makes a great substitute—great enough even to convert my tofuphobe husband, and, I hope, you, too.

How to serve: Light, pillowy, and versatile, Dutch baby is Sunday brunch sorted. It also makes a nice lunch entree. Pairs well with almost any kind of salad. Dutch baby is best right after it's made. Enjoy.

Ingredients

- 2 tablespoons olive oil or vegan butter
- 1 large onion, sliced
- 3 garlic cloves, coarsely chopped
- 8 ounces extra-firm tofu (half a 1-pound package), pressed, blotted dry, and coarsely chopped
- 1/4 cup aquafaba (the liquid from a can of chickpeas)
- 1/2 cup plain, unsweetened vegan yogurt*
- 2 tablespoons nutritional yeast
- 1/2 cup unbleached all-purpose flour or chickpea flour
- 1/2 teaspoon baking powder
- 1 handful fresh spinach leaves, chopped (optional)
- sea salt and fresh ground pepper
- 1 tablespoon fresh herbs, such as basil, dill, or sage, chopped
- 1/3 cup–1/2 cup optional toppings such as:
  ◊ fresh spinach leaves, chopped
  ◊ thinly sliced mushrooms
  ◊ thinly sliced peppers or onions
  ◊ halved grape tomatoes
  ◊ slender asparagus spears
  ◊ shredded vegan cheese

Instructions

- Preheat oven to 425°F.
- Heat olive oil or vegan butter in a large skillet over medium-high heat. Add the onion and stir. When it starts to soften, after a few minutes, add garlic. Reduce heat to medium and cook, stirring occasionally, until everything is soft and golden, 10–12 minutes.
- Set aside to cool.
- In a food processor, add chopped tofu, aquafaba, and vegan yogurt. Process briefly until smooth. Add sautéed onion, nutritional yeast, flour, and baking powder and process again, just until combined into a thick batter.
- Season generously with sea salt and freshly ground pepper. Stir in fresh spinach leaves, if using, and the fresh herbs. Spoon batter into a cast iron skillet or into a lightly oiled 8-inch baking dish. Smooth batter to spread evenly.
- Your Dutch baby is lovely and ready to bake just as it is, or decorate it with toppings of your choice. Resist the urge to crowd or overpopulate with toppings. Less is more.
- Bake for 15–20 minutes or until your Dutch baby is puffed, golden, and set. Slice and serve.
- Serves 2 to 4.

---

* I like plain unsweetened vegan yogurt in this for its subtle tang. You may substitute 1/2 cup plain unsweetened oat milk or other plant-based milk to which you add 1 tablespoon of cider vinegar. This will cause the milk to curdle and give you an approximation of vegan buttermilk.

Miami Favorites—Vegan Cheese Scones

I developed this scone recipe to bring to a brunch where I sensed (rightly) there'd be little else I could eat. They're rich, light, and tender with a delicate crust, yet quick and easy to make. I tripled the recipe (you can, too), so there was plenty to share, and honey, there was nothing left.

How to serve: Feel free to play with flavors. Add a tablespoon of basil, dill, or other finely chopped fresh herbs to the dough. Or skip the herbs and dry mustard and stir in 1/2 teaspoon of curry powder or cumin. Suitable for a lazy Sunday breakfast or fancy Mother's Day brunch, these scones also make fantastic apps, unbeatable with a glass of Champagne.

Ingredients

- 1/4 cup unsweetened oat milk
- 1 tablespoon cider vinegar
- 1 cup unbleached all-purpose flour
- 2 teaspoons baking powder
- 1/4 teaspoon baking soda
- 2 tablespoons nutritional yeast
- 1/4 teaspoon ground mustard
- 4 tablespoons (1/2 stick) vegan butter, chilled
- 1/2 cup grated or shredded vegan cheese of your choice
- 1-2 pinches sea salt

Instructions

- Preheat oven to 425°F. Line a baking sheet with a sheet of parchment or a Silpat.
- In a small bowl, mix together oat milk and cider vinegar. Mixture will clabber and become the tangy vegan equivalent of buttermilk. Set aside.
- In a large bowl or food processor, sift together flour, baking powder, baking soda, ground mustard, nutritional yeast, and sea salt. Work in the vegan butter gently and quickly, until the mixture forms coarse crumbs. Blend in clabbered oat milk and sea salt just until a dough forms.
- Lightly mix grated vegan cheese into the dough. You'll still see the cheese shreds, which will melt gorgeously into your scones as they bake.
- Turn out dough onto the baking sheet and lightly press into a 6-inch round. Use a knife to score the top to form six equal wedges. Option: top with another pinch of sea salt.
- Bake for 15 minutes, or until the kitchen smells cheesy and the edges of the scone round have turned golden brown. Cool briefly. The scones will easily separate into sixths.
- Serves 6.

Miami Favorites—Cat Head Biscuits

Cat head biscuits are big (cat-head-sized, if you're into hyperbole). Beloved all over the South, they're tall, fluffy, and alas, traditionally made with lard. This vegan version may upset Southern traditionalists, but their slight but pleasing tang and light texture honors the original without harm to pigs.

Ye olde biscuit-making hack—the cold vegan butter keeps the dough cool so the fat melts into the biscuit dough only during baking, making for pillow-light biscuits with a buttery taste. Many Southern cooks swear by White Lily flour, a soft wheat flour. I've adjusted by adding cornstarch to unbleached all-purpose flour to keep things light.

How to serve: Biscuits always taste best fresh out of the oven. Serve at once, while they're steaming hot. Split open and slather with vegan butter, your favorite jam, or vegan pimento cheese (p. 30).

Ingredients

- 1/2 cup unsweetened oat milk
- 1 tablespoon cider vinegar
- 1–3/4 cups unbleached all-purpose flour (plus additional for shaping biscuits)
- 3 tablespoons cornstarch
- 4-1/2 teaspoons baking powder
- pinch sea salt
- 6 tablespoons vegan butter, chilled
- 1 tablespoon vegan butter, melted (optional)

Instructions

- Preheat oven to 400°F. Line a rimmed baking sheet with parchment paper or Silpat.
- In a small bowl, whisk together oat milk and cider vinegar to make vegan buttermilk (the mixture will clabber—it's supposed to). Set aside.
- Use a light hand with the dough. Even better, use a food processor. Sift together flour, cornstarch, baking powder, and salt. Pulse a time or two to combine. Pulse in the cold vegan butter and mix quickly, just until the mixture becomes like coarse meal. Pour in vegan buttermilk and give a quick mix to form a damp dough.
- Dust the rolling surface generously with more flour. Turn out the biscuit dough. Knead oh-so-briefly, working in flour—a tablespoon or two at a time—just until dough loses its stickiness. Pat or roll out dough into a round about 1/2-inch thick. Flour the rim of a drinking glass or use a floured 2-inch or 3-inch biscuit cutter to form biscuits.
- Place biscuits on the rimmed baking sheet, spacing them so no one's crowded. Brush tops with melted vegan butter, if desired.
- Bake for 15 minutes. Biscuits should be lightly golden, pillowy, and fragrant.
- Makes about a dozen; serves 6 to 8.

Miami Favorites—Tofu Scramble or Almost Ackee

Ackee is a fruit tree originally from Africa, but it took to the Caribbean just fine. The fruit, when ripe, forms tender, golden curds, and cooks up buttery, like scrambled eggs. But here's the thing—it's toxic if you don't prepare it right. You can get properly cleaned and sorted ackee canned and packed in brine, but it doesn't offer the full flavor or charm of fresh ackee. It's cheaper and easier to use firm tofu instead. For those still of the *Eewwww, tofu* mindset, tofu scramble offers up the same soft, buttery curds as scrambled ackee or scrambled eggs.

I amp up my scramble with sautéed vegetables, so it's a hybrid scramble and vegetable hash. Feel free to change up any of the vegetables used here with what's fresh at your local farmers' market, but do aim for organic tofu—most soy out there is genetically modified.

How to serve: Nice with a couple of hot, fresh cat head biscuits (p. 8) or a heap of crispy hash browns as a breakfast or anytime treat. Tofu scramble can also serve as a wrap filling for a satisfying hand-held lunch. I like it every way with a splash of hot sauce.

Ingredients

- 12 ounces (about 3/4 of a 1-pound package) firm or extra-firm organic tofu, pressed and drained of excess water
- 1 tablespoon olive oil
- 1 small onion or 3 scallions, chopped
- 1 garlic clove, minced
- 1 jalapeño pepper, minced
- 1 red pepper, chopped, (about 1 cup)
- 1 small zucchini or yellow squash, chopped (about 1 cup)
- 1 teaspoon cumin
- 1/2 teaspoon turmeric
- 1 tablespoon nutritional yeast
- 1 tomato, chopped
- 1 handful fresh cilantro, chopped fine
- sea salt and fresh ground pepper to taste

Instructions

- Wrap tofu in a kitchen towel or paper towel to make sure it's good and dry.
- Heat olive oil in a large skillet over medium-high heat. Add chopped onion, jalapeño, red pepper, and zucchini. Stir and continue to cook for 7–10 minutes or until vegetables soften and turn golden and fragrant.
- Stir in cumin, turmeric, and nutritional yeast, coating vegetables well. Add chopped tomato and mix well.
- And now, the fun part. Crumble tofu into the skillet. You may mash it with a wooden spoon or enjoy the wonderfully tactile sensation of smooshing it between your fingers (a nice aggression release).
- Scramble everything together in merry fashion, breaking up any odd tofu clumps. Season generously with sea salt and ground pepper and continue cooking for about 3 minutes, until heated through. Mix in chopped cilantro and serve.
- Serves 2. Doubles like a dream.

Miami Flavors—French Toast with Caramelized Bananas

Your optimal lazy Sunday brunch dish.

How to serve: Dust with powdered sugar or drench with maple syrup, and maybe a dollop of coconut cream (p. 165). Garnish with sliced tropical fruits, a few strawberries. Or just enjoy as is.

Ingredients

- 2 cups plain unsweetened oat milk, full-fat coconut milk, or a combination
- 1/4 cup aquafaba
- 1 teaspoon vanilla
- 1 baguette, sliced in half widthwise and then into 6 planks, about 6 inches long
- 4 tablespoons (1/2 stick) vegan butter
- 1/2 cup brown sugar
- 3 bananas—ripe but not overripe, sliced lengthwise

Instructions

- In a wide, shallow bowl, whisk together the oat milk or coconut milk, aquafaba, and vanilla.
- Place the baguette slices in the milk, cut side down. Press gently so the bread soaks in all that goodness. Set aside and let the bread continue to absorb for another 15 minutes.
- Melt vegan butter in a large ovenproof skillet over medium-high heat.
- Using a spatula, lift the bread slices out of their milky bath and gently place them cut side down in the skillet. Sautée for about 5 minutes or so, until the bread is golden-brown and crusty underneath.
- Set the oven to broil.
- Gently turn the slices over. Place a banana slice on top of each slice of bread and scatter brown sugar over all.
- Place the skillet in the oven and broil for 5 minutes or so, until the brown sugar bubbles and the banana browns and caramelizes.
- Serve banana side up.
- Serves 6.

Miami Flavors—Tropical Granola

Granola started out in the 19th century as one of the first so-called health foods. By the 1960s, it had morphed into heartfelt, homemade hippie chow. Somewhere along the way, it became the mass-produced packaged commercial cereal that takes up an entire grocery store aisle. Granola has traveled far. Maybe too far. Though it still parades as being good for you, many brands contain buckets of sugar and fat. It's time to bring granola home.

Tropical granola has plenty of oaten goodness and coconut, pineapple, raisins, and warming spices for natural sweetness.

How to serve: Tropical granola goes down easy whether it's enjoyed at breakfast with plant-based milk or as a snack you gobble by the handful. Fancy it up by making a tropical granola parfait, layering granola, coconut yogurt, and chopped fresh fruit. The granola makes a lovely gift too. Pour into a Mason jar and dress it up with a pretty ribbon.

Ingredients

- 3 cups rolled oats*
- 1 cup dried unsweetened coconut flakes
- 1/2 cup raw cashews, chopped**
- 3 tablespoons sunflower seeds
- 2 tablespoons pumpkin seeds
- 2 tablespoons coconut oil
- 1/2 teaspoon cinnamon
- 1/2 teaspoon ginger
- 1/4 teaspoon nutmeg
- 1/4 teaspoon cardamom
- 4 tablespoons agave
- pinch sea salt
- 1/2 cup dried mango or pineapple, chopped or 1/2 cup banana chips
- 1/4 cup crystallized ginger, chopped
- 1/4 cup raisins

Instructions

- Preheat oven to 300°F. Spread parchment paper or Silpats on two rimmed baking sheets.
- In a large bowl, stir together oats, coconut, cashews, sunflower seeds, and pumpkin seeds. Then add the cinnamon, ginger, nutmeg, cardamom, and sea salt. Stir to combine. Then add the coconut oil and mix everything together.
- Spread granola on both baking sheets. Bake for 10 minutes, until things start to smell toasty.
- Remove the baking sheets from the oven, drizzle 2 tablespoons of agave on each baking sheet. Give everything a good toss. Now taste. If you like sweeter and stickier, add the other tablespoon of agave to each sheet pan. Mix well and spread out again, baking for another 20 minutes or until toasted and crunchy.
- Remove from the oven and allow to cool fully. Then store granola in an airtight container for up to 2 weeks.
- Makes 4 cups.

---

* Unsweetened oat flakes, also called old-fashioned oats. Instant oats will only let you down here.
** For those with nut allergies, double up on the pumpkin seeds or add hemp seeds. They both taste buttery and indulgent but offer lots of omega-3s and fiber. That's *real* health food.

Miami Flavors—Tropical Porridge

The English don't do summer well. "It's really just an idea," a gentleman told me one raw July morning in Bath. However, they do know their way around porridge (what we Yanks call oatmeal). While the concept of overnight oats has migrated to their side of the pond, a cup of cold, soupy oats on a chilly, wet day seems punishing. Most restaurants serve porridge the way I prefer to eat it—hot.

Steel cut oats, also known as pinhead oats, are the oats of choice here. They take longer to cook, but they're creamy, nutty-flavored, and filling. They're just the thing to power you through a miserable morning or prop you up when you're off your game.

Though fresh, local cherries, berries, apricots, and peaches were in season in Bath, I noticed they served their hot porridge topped with coconut and banana. Hey, that's *our* local fruit. But we can share. Oats have a natural affinity for these mild sweet fruits. I've upped the ante some by adding mango and starfruit, so you can enjoy a taste of the tropics wherever you are, even when summer is more of an idea.

How to serve: The mango, banana, and coconut should be gettable. Optional—give the banana slices a squeeze of lemon juice to keep them from oxidizing. Skip the starfruit if you don't have a neighbor with a tree.

Play up the tropical vibe with a shake of cinnamon and/or a dollop of whipped coconut cream (p. 165), or add your usual favorites, but resist the urge to get elaborate. It's breakfast and a comforting, fortifying one, at that.

If you're really into overnight oats, use rolled oats, Steel cut oats will get wet, but they will not soften, the plant-based milk will not thicken, and the result will make you wish you'd stayed in bed.

Ingredients

- 3 cups water
- 1 cup steel cut oats
- 1/2 cup unsweetened coconut flakes
- 1 banana, sliced into rounds
- 1 ripe mango, peeled and sliced
- 1 ripe starfruit, also called carambola, sliced lengthwise into star shapes
- squeeze of lemon for the banana, if desired

Instructions

- Bring the water to a boil in a saucepan. Pour in the oats and stir. Reduce heat to medium-high and continue stirring until the oats soak up the water and soften, becoming creamy but not mushy. Cook for 15–20 minutes until oatmeal optimization.
- While your oats cook, toast the coconut. Pour coconut flakes into a dry skillet. Heat over medium-high heat and toast, stirring occasionally for 3–5 minutes or until flakes turn golden-brown and smell buttery. Set aside.
- Divide hot oats into bowls and top with sliced banana, mango, and carambola. Finish with a sprinkling of toasted coconut flakes and serve at once.
- Serves 3 to 4. Doubles easily.

Miami Flavors—Summer Blueberry Loaf

The world loves a muffin, but a muffin, even the bakery ones as big as your head, is singular. A just-baked quick bread bursting with fresh fruit offers the possibility of more. You can cut the slices as skinny—or as generous—as you like.

I make a fruit-packed quick bread every week. Like the name says, it's quick and easy to make. There's no yeast involved, just baking powder or baking soda, to give the loaf its lift. Fruit quick bread is breakfast and/or afternoon pick-me-up for my husband and an anytime treat for us both. What I make depends on what's in season or what I've got handy—mango, banana, carrot, and pineapple, but blueberry bread is one of my faves.

Blueberries have the double benefit of being both virtuous (they're antioxidant and anti-inflammatory powerhouses) and delicious. They're mildly sweet and ever-so-slightly floral. In season, eat by the handful till your tongue turns blue (I do), add them to smoothies, and stock up, because extras freeze beautifully. But absolutely make this quick bread. It's moist, tender, and best of all, fruit-forward.

Ingredients

- 2 cups unbleached all-purpose flour
- 2/3 cup evaporated cane sugar
- 1-1/2 teaspoon baking powder
- 1 teaspoon baking soda
- 1 cup plain unsweetened vegan yogurt
- 2/3 cup fresh orange juice
- 1/4 cup grapeseed or other neutral oil
- 1 cup blueberries

Instructions

- Preheat oven to 375°F. Lightly oil a 9 × 5-inch loaf pan.
- In a large bowl, sift together unbleached flour, evaporated cane sugar, baking powder, and baking soda.
- In a separate bowl, whisk together vegan yogurt, orange juice, and grapeseed oil.
- Pour wet ingredients into the flour mixture and stir quickly, with a light hand, until just combined.
- Spoon the batter into the prepared loaf pan, and only then, sprinkle the blueberries on top, so the whole bread is studded with them.
- Bake for 1 hour or until the bread puffs and turns golden and springs back to the touch.
- Slices best when cool. Irresistible when warm. Freezes beautifully.
- If you absolutely must make muffins, prepare above, then spoon batter into a prepared muffin tin, filling cups 2/3 full. Bake for 20 minutes or until tops are puffed, pillowy, and golden-brown.
- Makes one loaf, serves 8 to 10.

Miami Favorites—Mango Quick Bread

Let me tell you something about baking with mango—it's tricky. Mango's succulent, sexy juiciness, when folded into a batter, can turn a cake into mush. The enzymes in mango don't play nice with flour. The secret, according to chef and cookbook author Deborah Madison, is to quiet the enzyme activity with baking soda. I can't explain the science behind it, but I can tell you it works (thanks, Deborah). I've adapted my mango bread from *New York Times*' baking queen Martha Rose Shulman's recipe for persimmon bread (thanks, Martha Rose). It's spice-driven rather than mango-forward, wellness-boosted with almond flour, and won't go to mush.

How to serve: This is one of many seasonal semi-good-for-you fruity quick breads I make for my husband. He eats them for breakfast with fresh fruit. A mid-afternoon slice (or two), lightly toasted, with a schmear or slather of nut butter is also welcome. Bread freezes well too.

Ingredients

- 1 cup mango purée (from about 1 fresh mango or use frozen mango, thawed)
- 2 teaspoons baking soda
- 1 cup whole wheat flour
- 1/2 cup unbleached all-purpose flour
- 3/4 cup almond flour
- 1 teaspoon cinnamon
- 1/2 teaspoon ginger
- 1/4 teaspoon nutmeg
- 1/4 teaspoon allspice
- 1/4 cup aquafaba
- 1/2 cup evaporated cane sugar
- 1/3 cup grapeseed or other neutral oil
- 1/3 cup unsweetened oat milk or other unsweetened plant-based milk
- 1 teaspoon vanilla
- 1/2 cup raisins or chopped dried mango

Instructions

- Preheat oven to 375°F. Lightly oil a 9 × 5-inch loaf pan.
- In a large mixing bowl or the bowl of a standing mixer or food processor, mix together the mango purée and 1 teaspoon baking soda. Set aside and let the mango purée thicken and undergo enzymatic transformation.
- In a separate bowl, sift together the remaining teaspoon of baking soda, whole wheat, all-purpose and almond flours, and the cinnamon, ginger, nutmeg, and allspice.
- Add to the mango mixture, the aquafaba, sugar, grapeseed oil, oat milk, and vanilla. Whisk together or mix on medium speed until well combined.
- Mix in about half the flour mixture and stir. Pour in the raisins or chopped dried mango, then the remaining flour. Mix again to form a thick batter.
- Pour into the prepared loaf pan. Bake for 50 minutes to an hour or until bread has risen, has a nice crust, and a toothpick inserted in the middle comes out clean. Cool on rack; then unmold and enjoy.
- Makes one loaf, serving 8.

Pastelitos de Guayaba—the Guava Pastry Backstory

Count among Cuba's gifts to Miami the pastelito. Literally little pastry, a pastelito is a flaky envelope of puff pastry. You can, in theory, fill it with almost anything, but in Miami, the filling of choice is guava and cream cheese, the tropical equivalent of peanut butter and jelly.

Guava trees, native to both Cuba and South Florida, produce a round fruit that fits in the palm of your hand. When ripe, the fruit gives off a sweetly floral fragrance almost like jasmine, with a faintly tangy top note. It's the scent of the tropics. The fruit itself is green on the outside, white or pink on the inside. The flesh is grainy, pectin-rich and contains a maddening number of tiny seeds.

Rather than painstakingly poking out the seeds, the flesh is pressed through a sieve then cooked down over low heat with a shocking amount of sugar—Cuba has a sweet tooth. Guava makes a killer jam. Keep the cooking and reduction going, though, and you get an especially dense version of jellied cranberry sauce in a can. It's the same garnet color, but without cranberry's tartness. It's formed into blocks, and *mira,* you've got guava paste, the must-have ingredient for guava and cream cheese pastry.

Better known here as pastelitos de guayaba, it's a delicious only-in-Miami mashup, where American innovation meets Latina cuisine. Back in Cuba, where they originated, the pastry was made with lard, and the cheese was queso fresco—simple farmer cheese. Here, commercial prepared puff pastry made the job easier, and the pastry just as flaky. Now queso fresco is in every Miami market, and probably yours as well. Before then, though, cream cheese was easier to come by, and wow, added that rich creaminess, too. It turned out to be an even better foil for guava. And then came quality commercial vegan cream cheese, and everyone was happy.

Miami Favorites—Guava Cream Cheese Pastry—Pastelitos de Guayaba

Puff pastry, vegan cream cheese, and guava paste, all gettable at your grocery store, come together for something easy to make, Instagram-worthy, and sublime to eat—crispy, flaky, creamy, sticky, and sweet in every bite.

How to serve: Pastelitos de guayaba are eaten at breakfast with a café Cubano and enjoyed throughout the day just because we can. Pastelitos taste best right out of the oven. They'll be snatched up for brunch, so make a double batch.

Ingredients

- 1 14-ounce package frozen puff pastry*
- 1 8-ounce package vegan cream cheese, chilled**
- 4 tablespoons powdered sugar
- 7–8 ounces guava paste (half a 14-ounce package)***

Instructions

- Preheat oven to 400°F. Line a rimmed baking sheet with a parchment sheet or Silpat.
- Unroll one sheet of puff pastry and fit onto the prepared baking sheet.
- In a small bowl, mix together the vegan cream cheese and powdered sugar until smooth and creamy. Powdered sugar contains a little cornstarch for lightness and structure. It helps the cream cheese here keep its shape and not go totally oozy on you.
- Pop the vegan cream cheese mixture in the freezer for a few minutes while you roll out the puff pastry.
- Take about half the brick of guava paste and slice it thinly, reserving the rest for another use.
- Spread cream cheese evenly on the bottom sheet of pastry, covering as much as possible and leaving just a little pastry bare at the edges.
- Fit the slices of guava paste on top, again covering as much as possible.
- Roll out the remaining sheet of puff pastry. Fit it on top of the guava and cream cheese. Gently press the edges of the pastry sheets together.
- Make diagonal slits across the top, about 2 inches apart, to let steam escape. Then lightly score the pastry into 16 individual pieces, but do not separate them.

---

* Choose frozen puff pastry sheets made with palm oil, not butter or, dios mio, lard.
** Different vegan cream cheese brands perform differently. Choose a kind that's firm, rather than spreadable. You can also omit the vegan cream cheese entirely; make all-guava pastries and get on with your life.
*** Guava paste is available in every Miami grocery store, many grocery stores throughout the country, online, and in specialty markets. Brands include Conchita and Iberia.

- Bake for 30 minutes or until pastry has puffed and turned a rich golden brown, and your kitchen smells buttery. Remove pastry from oven and allow it to cool.
- Slice through where you've scored the pastry. The pieces should separate easily.
- Makes 16 pastries, serving 8 to 12.

305 Pumpkin

Every autumn, friends up north flaunt their pumpkin pics on Instagram. Are we jealous? Hah. Florida has its own pumpkins. Calabaza, also known as Cuban, Jamaican, and Caribbean pumpkin, is happy to grow all across the Caribbean and Latin America, and right here in South Florida It's smaller than some of the other winter gourds, usually topping out at 12 pounds, but it loves our heat and humidity, whereas the jack o'lantern pumpkins shipped down for Halloween can go to mush in a day. Calabaza has a classic pumpkin shape with a dense shell. The outside is dusty green with white spots like paint spatters.

We also have our own native pumpkin, Seminole pumpkin. It's orange, thin-shelled, smaller, and sweeter than other pumpkins, including calabaza, and not too stringy, not too nasty. You may know Seminole as Miami's local tribe. The word means *in its natural place*.

Like other winter squash, calabaza and Seminole pumpkin go from brick hard when raw to creamy fleshed when cooked, with a mellow taste that whispers of warming spices and nuts. Their bright orange flesh signals high lutein and carotene levels. They're off-the-charts rich in fiber and vitamins A and C, good for glowing skin. Vitamin A boosts our collagen, the protein that keeps us sexy, not scraggy. It also boosts our neurotransmitters that keep our brains and bodies on good speaking terms.

So how do you get all that pumpkin goodness without damaging your chef's knife or yourself? With this spectacular hack: Pop your whole pumpkin in the oven at 350°F for about 10 minutes, or in the microwave for 30 seconds. It doesn't cook the pumpkin, but the heat softens it a little.

Let your gourd cool until it's easy to handle, then peel and chop it into manageable pieces. You can keep raw chopped pumpkin in a tightly sealed container in the refrigerator for several days.

Use the pumpkin cubes in
- sancocho (p. 101)
- pasta with pumpkin, lime, and annatto (p. 98).
- in place of sweet potato in the collard tacos (p. 105)

Smash it and make DIY pumpkin purée for:
- pumpkin bread (p. 28)
- Caribbean curried pumpkin dip (pumpkin talkari) (p. 26)

Pumpkin purée is doable in two ways, baking or steaming. Steaming is quicker; baking yields a slightly more intense, caramelized pumpkin. Like so much of life, it's a matter of tradeoffs.

To bake: Preheat oven to 350°F. Line a baking sheet with parchment paper. Cut pumpkin in half from top to bottom and scoop out seeds and stringy bits.

Place flesh side down on parchment and bake for 45–60 minutes until a knife is easily inserted and removed.

To steam: Pour a few inches of water into a large pot or the bottom half of a double boiler. Bring to boil. Place peeled and chopped pumpkin in the top half of a double boiler or a steamer basket insert. Cover and let the steam do its trick. This should take 15–20 minutes. You'll know the pumpkin is ready when the flesh pierces easily with a fork or knife blade.

To purée: Let the pumpkin cool, then spoon out the softened flesh. Tip the pumpkin into a food processor or high-speed blender and blitz for a minute or two or until it becomes velvety.

One extra step for perfect pumpkin purée: I like to set the purée in a strainer for 30 minutes or so, to let any excess liquid drain away. The result is more concentrated, more pumpkiny.

Pumpkin purée keeps refrigerated in an airtight container for a week or freeze it for several months. Or use it now for a little free spa treatment—pumpkin facial mask. Wash your face, pat dry, then spread the pumpkin purée on your face, avoiding the eye region. Let it sit for a few minutes till it starts to dry. The pumpkin enzymes zip off all kinds of impurities and tired skin. Then wash off and rinse clean and you'll see and enjoy the pumpkin glow.

Okay, yes, you can use canned pumpkin or frozen, thawed purée for these recipes, too. Do not use pumpkin pie filling, use 100% pumpkin, preferably organic.

Miami Favorites—Caribbean Curried Pumpkin Dip—Pumpkin Talkari

One thing Miami's figured out is that pumpkin means more than pie. Its natural sweetness shines in savory applications. Calabaza stars in sancocho (p. 101), a rich soup beloved throughout Latin America, in Haitian soupe joumou, and in pumpkin talkari, curried pumpkin dip from Trinidad. The gentle spices are Caribbean, but frizzling the spices and seeds in hot oil to bloom their flavor, a technique called tadka, is pure India.

How to serve: Slather on roti, stuff into collard leaves, or dredge up the dip with plantain chips and vegetables like celery sticks, sliced radishes, and raw or roasted cauliflower florets.

Ingredients

- 1-1/2 cups pumpkin purée (not pumpkin pie filling)
- 2 teaspoons Jamaican curry powder or your favorite curry blend*
- pinch sea salt plus more to finish
- 2 tablespoons coconut oil
- 1 thumb-sized piece of ginger, sliced into matchsticks
- 1/2 teaspoon fennel seed
- 1/2 teaspoon cumin seed
- 1/2 teaspoon nigella, also known as black onion seeds
- 1 cinnamon stick
- 1 sprig curry leaves, optional
- red pepper flakes, optional
- 2 teaspoons fresh lime juice (about 1/2 lime)
- sea salt to taste
- fresh greens for serving
- to garnish, any or all:
  - cilantro, chopped
  - pumpkin seeds
  - green sprouts
  - thyme leaves

Instructions

- Spoon your puréed pumpkin into a medium bowl. Stir in the curry powder and a good pinch sea salt. Set aside.
- In a small skillet, heat the coconut oil over medium-high heat. When it starts to shimmer, add the little slivers of ginger. Add the cumin, fennel and nigella seeds, cinnamon stick, and optional red pepper flakes and curry leaves, just for a minute or until curry leaves frizzle. Fish out the cinnamon stick and discard.
- Line a plate or shallow bowl with fresh greens. Spoon the pumpkin mash on top. Instead of going for smooth, dimple the surface all over with a chopstick or spoon handle. Drizzle the ginger, spices and seeds, then squeeze on the lime juice and add another pinch of sea salt.
- Accessorize with a scattering of pumpkin seeds, chopped cilantro, fresh sprouts, and/or thyme leaves.
- Serves 4 to 6.

Miami Flavors—Pumpkin Bread

I hate to break it to you, but there's no pumpkin in your seasonal pumpkin latte, just sweet warming spices like cinnamon and nutmeg. And sugar. Pumpkin is not just a latte flavor, it's more than pie, it's got a mellow, natural sweetness of its own. Capturing it's the tricky part.

I've tried many pumpkin bread recipes only to be disappointed with the results. Pumpkin's quiet charms can become even more hushed when lost in a batter. Pumpkin bread can be dry. Or soggy. Or heavy. Or oily. But rarely is it pumpkiny. So one day, I took an Ikea furniture assembly approach to pumpkin bread, trying this technique, that ingredient, a different proportion, and added a few weird tweaks of my own. It baked into the kind of bread to make a pumpkin proud. I did not, of course, write down the recipe. For the sake of the pumpkin and you, I had another go, recording as I went, and voila. The orange juice in this recipe is another gift from Florida. It doesn't announce itself in the least but adds a little sparkle of acidity. Think of that and the almond extract as accessorizing your pumpkin.

How to serve: This is a moist, fine-textured bread that slices well. It keeps for a week wrapped and refrigerated, or in the freezer for months. Nice for breakfast or afternoon snack just as it is or toasted. Enjoy it plain or gild with a schmear of nut butter. One friend fries slices in vegan butter. This does not earn a health halo but is probably yummy.

Ingredients

- 1 cup unbleached all-purpose flour
- 2/3 cup whole wheat flour
- 1 teaspoon baking soda
- 3/4 teaspoon baking powder
- 1 teaspoon cinnamon
- 1/4 teaspoon nutmeg
- 1/2 teaspoon ginger
- 1 cup homemade pureéd pumpkin (p. 109) or half a 14-ounce canned pumpkin
- 2 tablespoons aquafaba
- 1/3 cup molasses
- 1/4 teaspoon almond extract
- 1/2 cup raisins

Instructions

- Preheat oven to 350°F. Lightly oil 9 × 5-inch loaf pan.
- In a large bowl, sift together flours, baking soda, baking powder, and spices. Set aside.
- In a smaller separate bowl, stir together pumpkin purée, orange juice, aquafaba, and molasses.
- In another large bowl, beat vegan butter and sugar until light. Add about half the flour and spice mixture, then stir in half the pumpkin mixture. Repeat with the remaining flour and pumpkin. Keep it light. Stir in the raisins.
- Spoon batter into loaf pan. Bake for 1 hour, or bread is until fragrant and firm. It should spring back with a gentle poke.
- Makes one loaf, serving 8 to 10.

Miami Favorites—Smoked Sea Dip

Sitting by Biscayne Bay with a scoop of smoked fish dip and an ice cold beer has long been one of Miami's great pleasures. Unless you're (1) a fish or (2) vegan.

Without hard evidence to back me up, I believe smoked fish dip's origins go back to the Seminole and Miccosukee, who taught early settlers the technique of smoking food. It not only added umami and balanced out the flavor of some of the stronger-tasting local fish like wahoo (don't you just love the name?), it also served as a preservative. Refrigerators wouldn't come along for a century or so, and having smoked fish on hand meant there was always something to eat.

This dip offers all the pleasure, smokiness, and brininess of the original, yields plenty to eat, and leaves the fish and our imperiled marine life in peace. It needs but 5 minutes and 5 ingredients. Tempeh, an undersung fermented soy cake high in protein, and canned artichoke hearts, that salad bar staple, provide a very close approximation of fish's flakiness, the nori supplies the sea flavor, the liquid smoke adds that deep, savory taste, and the vegan mayo holds everything together.

How to serve: Smoked fish dip is usually served with carrot and celery sticks, which no one eats, and crackers—we're talking Saltines or similar—to serve as plinths for your dip.

However, since we're already breaking with tradition by leaving the fish out of the equation, you can also use the smoked sea dip as a sandwich filling, topped with lettuce, tomato, and onion. I could even imagine eating this on a bagel. Enjoy as a dip or in a sandwich, but serve it with hot sauce for splashing and lemon quarters for squeezing.

Ingredients

- 1 cup artichoke hearts, rinsed and drained—you want canned or frozen here, not the oily marinated ones in a jar
- 8 ounces (1 package) tempeh, available in most grocery stores in the refrigerated section right next to the tofu
- 1 teaspoon nori dust (recipe p. 121)
- 1 teaspoon liquid smoke
- 2 tablespoons vegan mayonnaise, available in the refrigerated section of most grocery stores, possibly even near the tempeh and tofu

Instructions

- Pour drained artichoke hearts into a food processor. Crumble in the tempeh. Pulse briefly to break everything up to a chunky but uniform consistency, kinda like tuna salad, not a homogenized paste. Alternatively, bash artichoke hearts and tempeh with a large heavy spoon.
- Add nori dust, liquid smoke, and vegan mayo and process again. Taste and get it as you like.
- Feel free to add more nori dust 1/4 teaspoon at a time, if you want fishier, a dash more liquid smoke if you want smokier, and another good dollop of vegan mayonnaise if you want creamier.
- Serves 4 to 6.

Miami Favorites—Vegan Pimento Cheese

OG pimento cheese, made of mayonnaise, cheese, and pimento, is two-thirds horrible for you. Everyone loves it. Except vegans. This recipe has a few more ingredients than the dairy and egg-loaded classic, but all ingredients are available and accessible. It comes together in minutes, it's retro-chic, and as any maker of pimento cheese, vegan or otherwise will tell you, my recipe's the best.

- whole food plant-based
- oil-free
- soy-free
- gluten-free

How to serve: It's tempting to scoop up and eat straight out of the food processor, but cover and chill for at least an hour. This allows the flavors to develop and deepen. The cheese will firm up some too, becoming more of a lush cream cheesy consistency. Enjoy as a sandwich filling or scoop up with raw vegetables or for an elevated vegan pimento cheese experience, serve with cat head biscuits (p. 8).

Ingredients

- 8 ounces raw cashews soaked overnight*
- 3 tablespoons nutritional yeast
- 1 teaspoon apple cider vinegar
- 1 teaspoon paprika
- 1/4 teaspoon turmeric
- 2 pimentos—canned or jarred work fine—plus a little of their juice
- a squeeze of fresh lemon juice (about a teaspoon)
- sea salt and fresh ground pepper to taste
- optional adds:
    - splash of hot sauce or pinch cayenne
    - 1/2 teaspoon white miso
    - 1/2 teaspoon garlic powder

Instructions

- Drain and rinse cashews. Pour into a food processor and whiz or pulse until you've got a thick paste.
- Add remaining ingredients:
    - nutritional yeast for cheesiness
    - apple cider vinegar for the littlest bit of acidic edge
    - paprika to deepen flavor
    - turmeric for a little bit of earthy funk and to nail that adorable pale orange shade
    - pimento—you cannot make pimento cheese without pimento
- Blitz it all together for 3–5 minutes or until it's luscious, totally smooth with no graininess from the nuts, and you've achieved that particular pimento cheese shade.
- Squeeze in fresh lemon juice and taste. Add any optional ingredients—the miso, hot sauce and/or garlic powder. Season with sea salt and fresh pepper, and taste again for balance.
- Serves 4 to 6.

---

* Got nut allergies? Substitute 1/2 cup sunflower seeds and 1/2 cup pumpkin seeds for the cashews.

Miami Favorites—Hoecakes

Primal, economical, and belly-filling, hoecakes are corn cakes at their simplest. They're crispy on the outside, tender on the inside. They're not fluffy, they're not fritters, they're not fancy. They're not meant to be. But humble as they are, they inspire passion. As Mark Twain's Huckleberry Finn notes, "There ain't nothing in the world so good when it's cooked right."

How to serve: Serve with your favorite jam or vegan butter or plain with a pinch of sea salt, but get 'em while they're hot, right out of the skillet.

Ingredients

- 2 cups cornmeal
- 1 teaspoon sea salt, plus more to finish
- 1-1/2 cups boiling water
- 2–3 tablespoons olive oil or grapeseed oil or other neutral oil

Instructions

- Combine cornmeal and salt in a medium-sized mixing bowl. Slowly pour in boiling water in a stream, stirring constantly until the batter is thick but without lumps. It'll look a little like scrambled eggs.
- Set aside for at least 10 minutes to let the batter coalesce.
- Meanwhile, heat skillet, preferably cast iron, over high heat until hot. Pour in one tablespoon of oil. When it starts to shimmer, drop in dollops of hoecake batter, about a tablespoon each, and spread to make 4-inch rounds.
- Cook 2–3 minutes; then flip and cook for another few minutes. Hoecakes should be golden brown, crispy, and a little lacy at the edges. Add more oil as needed to the skillet for the remaining batter.
- Serve at once with a final sprinkle of sea salt.
- Makes about a dozen, serving 4.

Miami Favorites—Cornbread

Cornbread can be contentious. Do you make it with white cornmeal or yellow? Do you add sugar? Do you like it custardy or cakey? Oh, why argue? Cornbread is where the Caribbean, Latin America, and the American South come together—we all love it.

How to serve: Let cool slightly after baking to prevent crumbling. Enjoy warm with vegan butter, with greens, beans, and to soak up the goodness of Haitian sos pwa (p 68).

Ingredients

- 7 tablespoons vegan butter
- 1-1/2 cups cornmeal, whatever color you want, even blue
- 1 cup unbleached all-purpose flour
- 2 tablespoons sugar
- 1 teaspoon sea salt
- 1 tablespoon baking powder. Yeah, it seems like a lot. Trust me.
- 1/4 cup aquafaba
- 1-1/2 cups unsweetened oat milk

Instructions

- Preheat oven to 400°F.
- Place vegan butter in a 9-inch ovenproof skillet or baking dish and place in the oven to melt, about 8 minutes, long enough to make the rest of the cornbread batter.
- In a large bowl, sift together cornmeal, unbleached flour, sugar, salt and baking powder. Pour in the plant-based milk, aquafaba, and about half the melted vegan butter, leaving the rest of it in the baking dish.
- Stir wet ingredients into dry, using a light hand until just combined. Batter will be thick. Spoon into the prepared baking dish.
- Bake for 25–30 minutes. Cornbread is done when it's risen, smells buttery, and has formed a tawny crust that demands a nibble or two. It should spring back after a gentle poke.
- Serves 6 to 8.

Succulence—Juicy, Fresh, Ripe Tastes of the Tropics

Magic Dust

One of Miami's hottest commercial spice blends is Tajin, a blend of cumin, chile, dried lime, and salt from Mexico. This flavor combination—funky, fiery, tart, and salty—is also a core flavor principal across the Middle East, where the lime is nudged out by sumac, a tart berry, and in India, where the tartness comes from amchoor, dried mango powder. Anything mango you'd think would be sweet, but amchoor is made from green, underripe mango, and it's mouth-puckeringly tart. It's also beloved in Latin and Caribbean cuisines, making it a Miami meant-to-be.

They call it Tajin spice in Mexico, chaat masala in India, but in my kitchen, it's known as magic dust. Sprinkle it generously on popcorn, or use it to punch up the flavors in anything from feijoada (p. 85) to fruit. Yes, fruit. A sprinkle of magic dust, and your fruit is transformed, as though on HD. Magic!

No amchoor? No problem. Finish your dish with a squeeze of fresh lime juice.

Miami Favorites—Magic Dust

Ingredients

- 1/2 teaspoon cumin
- 1/4 teaspoon chile powder
- 1/2 teaspoon amchoor or sumac
- * pinch of sea salt

Instructions

- In a dry skillet, toast cumin and chile over medium heat just for a minute or two until spices warm and release their fragrance.
- Pour cumin and chile into a small bowl or ramekin. Add sea salt and stir.

---

* Available at specialty markets and online.

Miami Flavors—Magic Dust Tropical Fruit Plate

Tropical fruits like papaya, mango, banana, pineapple, oranges, grapefruit, and strawberries are wonderful here, but so are orchard fruits like peaches, plums, nectarines, and pears. Almost any fruit'll do here, and the more colors, textures, and flavors, the better. Just remember fruits that oxidize quickly, like apples and bananas, can go brown and mushy, so add them just before serving (and maybe give them a squeeze of lemon juice to keep flavor and color bright). Don't forget the magic dust.

How to serve: I know you're all into cooking shows and boards on Instagram, but fruit is juicy and acidic. A china or ceramic platter will serve you better here. But do summon your inner food stylist. Fruit, with its naturally bright colors and pretty shapes, makes styling easy.

Don't want to bother? Mix the fruit together in a bowl, add magic dust, and stir. Magic dust fruit plate is best enjoyed as soon as it's assembled. It's a delicious lesson in enjoying the moment.

Ingredients

- 5 cups local, seasonal fruit and its ripest and most luscious, chopped or sliced
- 1 batch of magic dust
- 1 good squeeze of fresh lime juice
- optional finishes:
    - 2 tablespoons toasted cashews or pistachios
    - 2 tablespoons crystallized ginger, chopped
    - 1 handful mint leaves or microgreens

Instructions

- Arrange fruit on a platter. Accessorize with nuts and chopped ginger. Garnish with the mint or microgreens. Finish by sprinkling on the magic dust, and squeeze on the lime juice if you need it. Serve at once.
- Serves 4 to 6.

Miami Flavors—Sheet Pan Panzanella with Charred Summer Vegetables and Cornbread Croutons

Panzanella, Italy's classic summer salad, makes brilliant use of fresh tomatoes and stale bread, offering big flavor and little waste. Taking the same idea to the South, we keep the juicy, ripe tomatoes but add an abundance of charred summer produce, dress it with remoulade, and top it all with toasted cornbread croutons.

Remoulade sauce sounds rarified and elegant, but honey, it's fancied-up mayonnaise, so easy to make vegan. The creamy, slightly zesty sauce makes summer vegetables—even underloved okra and summer squash—sing.

Roast the vegetables in the oven, or for extra smoky flavor, grill them outside. Either way, this seasonal salad comes together fast and fabulous.

How to serve: You can serve this as a side salad, but it can easily be a meal all on its own. It's delicious but not built to last. Enjoy the moment, darling.

The dressing makes more than you'll need for the salad, so serve the extra on the side for those who like their salads extra creamy.

Ingredients

- 2 tablespoons olive oil, divided use
- 1 onion, sliced in half and again into skinny half-moons (about 3/4 cup)
- 1 summer squash or zucchini, sliced horizontally (about 1-1/2 cups)
- 1/2 pound okra (about a dozen), preferably small ones, sliced in half lengthwise
- 3 cloves garlic, chopped
- 1 red pepper, sliced (about 1 cup)
- 1 tablespoon lemon juice
- 4 cups fresh greens, such as arugula, spinach, or butter lettuce
- 12 grape tomatoes, halved
- sea salt and fresh ground pepper
- 1-1/2 cups cornbread* into 1-inch cubes, from a good-sized wedge. Slightly stale is fine and is a delicious way to reduce food waste.

Remoulade

- 1/3 cup vegan mayonnaise
- 1 tablespoon Dijon or Creole whole grain mustard

---

* My vegan cornbread recipe works great here (p. 34) and leaves you plenty of extra for other meals.

- 1 teaspoon Creole or blackened spice**
- 1 teaspoon fresh lemon juice
- 2 teaspoons capers, rinsed, and drained

Instructions

- Preheat oven to 425°F. Line 2 rimmed baking sheets with parchment sheets or Silpats.
- Spread the sliced onion, summer squash, and okra onto one of the prepared baking sheets, making sure not to crowd the vegetables. Drizzle on 1 tablespoon of the olive oil and the lemon juice, giving okra special attention. Lemon's acidity prevents the okra going limp and lubed on you. Sprinkle the vegetables with a pinch of sea salt and roast for 10 minutes.
- In the meantime, slice the pepper, slice the cornbread, and place on the second rimmed baking sheet. Drizzle with the remaining tablespoon of olive oil and sprinkle with a pinch of sea salt.
- Stir or flip the okra and summer squash so they roast evenly. Return to oven, then reduce heat to 400°F. Place the sheet pan of pepper and cornbread cubes in the oven.
- Continue roasting both sheet pans for another 15–20 minutes or until everything smells toasty and the vegetables have a slight char.
- In a small bowl, whisk together all the remoulade ingredients until combined.
- Paint about half the remoulade on the bottom of a serving platter or shallow bowl.
- Mound fresh greens on top. Scatter the charred vegetables on top of the greens, then add the sliced grape tomatoes. Finish with the cornbread croutons, a few flakes of sea salt, and a good grinding of pepper. Serve extra dressing on the side.
- Serves 4.

** Creole seasoning is a blend of spices including garlic, paprika, cayenne, and possibly, a whole host of others, including turmeric, celery seed., and often a whole lot of salt. It's available commercially, but here's an easy but elemental DIY version:
In a small bowl or ramekin, mix together:
- 1 teaspoon paprika
- 1 teaspoon garlic powder
- 1-2 pinches cayenne

Use only 1 teaspoon of the spice mix for the remoulade, reserving the rest in a small airtight container to enjoy in other Creole recipes.

Miami Flavors—Fireworks Black Bean and Mango Salad

I created this recipe a few years ago to bring to my friend D's annual Fourth of July party. I wasn't planning to, but that day, she called and said, "Hey, are you still vegan?" Um, yeah, now and forever. The party spread turned out to be not vegan-friendly, and D asked if I could bring something that was. So with little warning, and using what I had in the kitchen, I came up with a winner.

Fireworks Black Bean and Mango Salad combines tender, earthy-flavored black beans, sweet, juicy mango, tart lime, sweet and hot peppers, soft, fresh greens, and buttery toasted pepitas—pumpkin seeds—offer healthy fats and fun crunch. It's a no-cook wonder that can sit out on a picnic table for hours without wilting.

Oil-free fans, this is your moment. And even if you're not oil-free, this is your salad. It's naked—in a sexy way, I hope—but I mean it doesn't have a real dressing. It doesn't need it. The cumin, lime juice, and mango create the flavor, and the mango also provides the right amount of moisture that holds everything together. These flavors, textures, and colors come together like a burst of fireworks. Like America itself.

How to serve: Great as part of a buffet or picnic. Nice with cornbread (p. 34) or hoecakes (p. 32).

Ingredients

- 1 jalapeño, minced
- 1 red pepper, diced (about 1 cup)
- 2 stalks celery chopped fine (about 1 cup)
- 2 15-ounce cans black beans rinsed and drained or 4 cups cooked black beans
- 1 teaspoon cumin
- juice of 1/2 lime (about 1 tablespoon)
- 2 mangos, peeled and diced (about 2 cups)
- 1 bunch cilantro chopped
- sea salt and fresh ground pepper to taste
- 1/4 cup toasted pepitas pumpkin seeds for garnish, optional but adding fabulous crunch, not to mention goodly amounts of manganese and magnesium
- 3–4 cups fresh greens like spinach, arugula or frisée

Instructions

- In a large bowl, gently mix together jalapeño, diced red pepper, and celery. Add the black beans and combine well.
- Add the cumin and the lime and toss to coat.
- Just before serving, add the chopped mangos and chopped cilantro to the black beans. Season to taste. Place black beans and mango atop greens and serve at once, garnishing with toasted pepitas, if you like (and you will).
- Serves 4.

Miami Flavors—Green Mango Salad

Like jackfruit and papaya, mango can live two lives. Ripe mango gets all the buzz and love, but not every mango is destined for sweet, sticky, golden glory. Green mango has a glory of its own. Green, unripe mango is like it sounds—green-skinned, with pale, firm flesh which has a mild, vegetal flavor and slight astringency. Embrace it. Better yet, eat it. Local-as-anything produce—mango, jicama, cabbage, lemongrass, chili, mint, ginger, and cilantro—tumble together to create a cooling salad bright with Asian flavors.

Can't find jicama aka Mexican turnip? Substitute another crunchy vegetable such as radish, daikon, carrot, or kohlrabi.

How to serve: Green mango salad makes a crisp, light spirit-lifting lunch. You can also serve green mango salad with dim sum, fried rice, your favorite slurpy Asian noodles—or all of it for a fabulous feast.

Ingredients

- 1 cup green mango, sliced into matchsticks
- 1/2 cup jicama, sliced into matchsticks
- 1 cup cabbage, shredded
- 8 ounces extra-firm or firm tofu (half a 1-pound package) pressed to expel excess water, blotted dry, and sliced into matchsticks
- 2 tablespoons lime juice
- 2 tablespoons soy sauce
- 1 teaspoon coconut sugar or evaporated cane sugar
- 1 serrano or other green chile with a little spirit and sting, minced
- 1 tablespoon fresh lemongrass, minced or 1 teaspoon lemongrass powder
- 1 teaspoon fresh ginger, minced
- 1 clove garlic, minced
- sea salt to taste
- 1/3 cup cilantro, chopped
- 1/4 cup mint leaves, chopped
- 1/3 cup roasted peanuts, chopped

Instructions

- In a large bowl, mix together green mango, jicama, and cabbage. If you're doing this ahead (and you can), cover and refrigerate for several hours.
- In a small separate bowl, whisk together lime juice, soy, and sugar. Stir until sugar dissolves. Add minced serrano, lemongrass, ginger, and garlic, and give a stir. Add the pressed tofu and let it marinate.
- When ready to serve, pour the dressing and tofu over the green mango and vegetables. Mix everything together with a light hand. Add a pinch of sea salt. Sprinkle on the cilantro and mint. Mix again and taste, adding more salt if desired.
- Mound on a communal platter—very stylish—or spoon into individual bowls. Scatter chopped peanuts on top.
- Serves 4.

Sofrito Vs Choka

Both sofrito and choka are made with onions, peppers, and garlic sautéed in olive oil so they're rich and full-flavored. So what's the difference? Oh, honey, plenty. Sofrito hails from Miami's Latin side—Puerto Rico, Dominican Republic and the like. Choka tilts Trini (from Trinidad) and the Caribbean.

Sofrito is used to build flavor in dishes, like chickpeas with saffron (p. 81), or even sukuma wiki (p. 128). Sofrito is meant to play a supporting role. Choka is a star in and of itself. It's the main attraction, enjoyed as is or with the simple addition of crushed roasted eggplant or tomato. Fun fact—choka is also a formal style of Japanese poetry dating back to the sixth century. Trini choka isn't formal, it's fun, but with bold flavor that bespeaks a poetry of its own.

And the good news is, you don't have to choose between sofrito and choka. We enjoy both in Miami, and you can, too.

Miami Flavors—Tomato Choka

If you like Caribbean curried pumpkin dip (p. 26), you'll love tomato choka. Both are glorious Trini mashups—quite literally—of salad and salsa. Tomato choka involves grilling or roasting tomatoes until they're pretty close to burnt. Then they're smashed and tossed with sautéed onions, garlic, chile, and ginger.

How to serve: It's tempting to eat tomato choka spooned right out of the pan—I've done it—but it's also good scooped up with roti, served with hoecakes (p. 32) or crispy grits cakes (p. 134)), or make it part of a significant salad, like arugula with tomato choka and chickpea tofu (p. 49).

If the flavor of coconut rocks your world, substitute coconut oil for olive oil.

Ingredients

- 1 pint grape or cherry tomatoes
- 1 tablespoon olive oil or coconut oil
- 1 small onion, sliced in half; then sliced into skinny half-moons (about 1 cup)
- 3 cloves garlic, minced
- 1 sliver Scotch bonnet pepper or 1/2 jalapeño, minced
- 1 thumb-sized piece of ginger, minced
- sea salt to taste
- juice of 1 fresh lime
- 1/4 cup cilantro, chopped

Instructions

- Preheat oven to 425°F. Line a rimmed baking sheet with parchment or a Silpat.
- Spill grape tomatoes onto the baking sheet, spreading them out so as not to crowd. Roast for 25 minutes or until tomatoes have a nice blister/char thing going. Remove from oven and let cool.
- In a large skillet, heat the olive or coconut oil over medium-high heat until it shimmers.
- Add the sliced onion and stir to coat the onion in oil. then reduce heat to medium. After about 5 minutes, the onions should soften and turn translucent, edging toward pale gold. Add minced garlic, minced ginger, and minced Scotch bonnet or jalapeño. Continue cooking, stirring occasionally, until the vegetables are relaxed and fragrant.
- Tip the roasted tomatoes into the sautéed vegetables. Bash tomatoes with a large wooden spoon so they burst, creating a textured, chunky choka. Give everything a good stir. Season with sea salt and fresh lime juice.
- Pour choka into a bowl and leave at room temperature for about an hour, allowing flavors to combine. Just before serving, stir in the cilantro and taste again, adding more sea salt or lime juice, if desired.
- Serves 4. Recipe doubles easily.

Miami Flavors—Tomato Choka Salad with Chickpea Tofu

There's a reason why the chain of islands between Florida and South America is called the West Indies. Many of the islands have large Indian communities going back generations, and their influence can be seen, felt, and tasted. Taste it here in this main course salad, a Caribbean, deconstructed vegan version of palak paneer, India's classic spinach curry. Fresh, peppery arugula stands in for palak paneer's cooked puréed spinach, and spiced chickpea tofu is a change-up for paneer (India's version of farmer's cheese). Tomato choka (p. 48) is the secret sauce that makes it sing. Or zing.

About that chickpea tofu—there's no tofu involved, just chickpea flour and water. It takes less than 10 minutes to make, then let chill in the refrigerator for an hour or so before baking. We all need time to chill. The result is lightly spiced, savory, and not at all like tofu. Chickpea tofu is firm on the outside, fluffy, soft, and yielding within. It's lighter than hummus, and unlike hummus, there's no tahini or oil, except for the little brushed on before baking.

How to serve: Serve this significant salad while the chickpea tofu is still warm, and with the tomato choka at room temperature. A meal unto itself, it can also be served with curried pumpkin dip (p. 26), Caribbean curry (p. 112) and a warm stack of roti, griddled whole wheat flatbread.

Besides this salad, you can enjoy chickpea tofu as part of your favorite grain and vegetable bowl. It also pairs well with coconut green beans (p. 140). Omit the garam masala if you're going to spin the dish away from the West Indies.

The chickpea tofu and tomato choka may be made ahead and kept separately, so you can assemble the salad in minutes.

Not into arugula? Substitute tender mustard greens or watercress, something with a little kick. Not into kicks? Fresh spinach or lettuce'll work, too.

Ingredients

For the chickpea tofu:
- 1 cup chickpea flour*
- 1–3/4 cups water
- sea salt
- 1 teaspoon garam masala
- 1/2 teaspoon cumin
- 1 tablespoon olive oil or coconut oil for drizzling
- 6 cups arugula or other greens
- 1 recipe tomato choka (p. 48)
- chopped cilantro for garnish

---

* Chickpea flour is available at many grocery stores in the baking aisle, as well as specialty markets and online.

- optional adds:
  - roasted eggplant, zucchini, and/or cauliflower
  - blanched green beans
  - sprouts
  - sliced avocado
  - chopped, roasted cashews
  - thinly sliced radishes

Instructions

- Lightly oil a 9 × 5-inch loaf pan.
- Make the chickpea tofu. In a bowl, whisk together the chickpea flour, water, sea salt, garam masala, and cumin until you have a pale smooth, lump-free batter.
- Pour batter into a medium saucepan and heat over medium-high heat, stirring frequently. After about 5 minutes, the batter will thicken and start to seize up. Keep beating to keep things smooth and avoid sticking. If the mixture starts to boil, reduce heat to medium and continue stirring and cooking until it reaches the consistency of thick, velvety hummus, about 3 minutes more.
- Spoon batter into prepared loaf pan. It will only fill the pan halfway. Using the back of a spoon, smooth the top. Allow the batter to cool, then cover tightly and refrigerate for at least an hour. The chickpea tofu will continue to firm up in the fridge.
- Preheat oven to 350°F.
- Line a rimmed baking sheet with parchment paper or a Silpat.
- Remove chickpea tofu from the fridge and uncover. If it's produced any liquid, don't fret, it's okay. Blot the top lightly with a paper towel, and you're good.
- Slice chickpea tofu into 1-inch cubes. It will still be soft but should hold its shape. Spread cubes on the baking sheet. Drizzle lightly with olive or coconut oil. Give another sprinkle of sea salt.
- Bake for 30 minutes, then give the chickpea tofu a gentle prod. It should feel firm but not dense, and start to darken at the edges. Remove from oven and allow to cool slightly.
- Set aside tomato choka, allowing it to come to room temperature.
- Mound arugula or other greens in a bowl or platter. Tumble the tofu on top, add any extras, then spoon tomato choka over all. Serve at once.
- Serves 4 to 6.

Miami Flavors—Seven Seed Quinoa with Spinach and Sesame Dressing

In honor of Seed Food and Wine, Miami's premiere vegan food festival, I created this quick and easy quinoa dish, sparked with seeds and citrus and tossed with a luscious tahini dressing.

How to serve: I've said it before, I'll say it again—not all salad needs to be icebox cold. Here, the flavors bloom when it's served a few degrees warmer, more toward room temperature. It's got layers of tastes and textures, not to mention nutritional goodness enough to qualify as a main event. However, you can also enjoy as a significant salad or as the heart of a quinoa bowl topped with delights like chickpea tofu (p. 49) and slices of roasted winter squash, or spoonfuls of tropical slaw (p. 58). Drizzle on some extra tahini sauce and you're in business.

Ingredients

- 1 cup vegetable broth or water
- 1 cup orange juice
- 1 cup quinoa
- 1 tablespoon olive oil
- 1 tablespoon cumin seeds
- 1 tablespoon fennel seeds
- 1 tablespoon hemp seeds
- 1 tablespoon sesame seeds
- 2 tablespoons sunflower seeds
- 3 tablespoons pumpkin seeds
- pinch red pepper flakes (if desired)
- 6 cups fresh spinach leaves, chopped
- 1/3 cup pomegranate seeds

For the sesame dressing:

- 1/3 cup orange juice
- 1 clove garlic, minced
- 1/2 teaspoon turmeric
- 2 tablespoons tahini
- sea salt and fresh ground pepper

Instructions

- In a medium saucepan, bring broth or water and orange juice to boil over high heat. Pour in quinoa. Stir to combine, reduce heat to low, then cover. Let quinoa cook for 25–30 minutes or until all the liquid is absorbed and the quinoa grains release their endosperm tails. Remove the lid and set aside to cool.
- Meanwhile, make the sesame dressing. In a small saucepan over medium heat, warm orange juice and minced garlic until just warmed through. Add turmeric and tahini and whisk. At first, the mixture will look curdled. Continue to whisk for another 2–3 minutes or until it turns smooth and thickens to a custard-like consistency. Season generously with sea salt and pepper.
- Spoon half of the dressing—about 3 tablespoons—into the quinoa and gently stir to combine. The recipe may be prepared a day or two in advance at this point, then kept covered and refrigerated. Bring back to room temperature to finish.
- In a small skillet, heat olive oil over medium-high heat. Add cumin, fennel, hemp, sesame, sunflower, and pumpkin seeds,

plus the red pepper flakes, if desired. Stir and toast for 2–3 minutes, until seeds begin to toast and become fragrant. Pour onto quinoa and give a stir or two to fluff and combine. Season generously with sea salt and pepper.

- Add the chopped spinach by the handful and toss again. Season to taste with sea salt and pepper and mix in another spoonful of dressing, if desired. Garnish by scattering the pomegranate seeds on top.
- Serves 6.

Greens

You know Florida for citrus, but we're so much more. Including greens. Collards, kale, lettuce, chard, escarole, callaloo, cabbage, turnip greens, mustard greens, dandelion greens, microgreens, radish and carrot tops, and more, more, more exploding from the farmers market kiosks, overwhelming your CSA box and taking over your fridge.

These recipes help you reclaim the precious real estate inside your refrigerator and are so easy and flavorful you may come to feel as I do—you can never have too many greens.

Miami Flavors—Catalan Spinach

Take a handful of accessible ingredients, and in just 5 minutes, you have my favorite tapas dish. Catalan spinach is naturally vegan, and the addition of dried fruit and nuts is an old Mediterranean technique that makes greens easier to love. It works. It's a great gateway to get more greens in your life.

How to serve: Beautiful as part of a whole tapas table, but also as an accompaniment to another Catalunian classic gone vegan Chickpeas with Saffron (p. 81).

Ingredients

- 1/4 cup raisins
- 1 garlic clove, minced
- 2 teaspoons olive oil
- 1/4 cup pine nuts, pistachios, or chopped almonds
- 6 cups spinach, chopped
- 2 teaspoons sherry vinegar
- sea salt and fresh ground pepper

Instructions

- Pour raisins in a small bowl and cover with warm water. This plumps them up. Let them sit.
- Heat olive oil in a large skillet over medium-high heat. Mince garlic clove and add, cooking briefly, just until the garlic starts to turn golden and fragrant. Drain raisins and add them to the skillet.
- Then add the nuts. Stir so they toast, just for a minute or two.
- Now add your chopped spinach by the handful. Turn off the heat, stir, and let the spinach wilt just slightly. The leaves should remain bright green.
- Splash in the sherry vinegar, stir for another minute, and season with sea salt and fresh ground pepper.
- Serves 3 to 4. Doubles easily.

Miami Flavors—Miami Beet Salad

Beets, fennel, walnuts—an elegant trio made for each other. Bring citrus, sprouts, tahini, and pomegranate seeds to the party, and the elegant trio gets to have a little fun for a change. If red beets are too much for you, look for golden beets. They're milder in flavor. Either way, the colors and shapes in this salad make for optimal eye appeal.

How to serve: This is cause for a composed salad, where the ingredients are arranged rather than tossed (though you can do that too). Plated, it should look like a giant blossom.

Ingredients

- 1 whole large beet or two small greens trimmed and reserved for another use (about 1-1/2 cups)
- 1 large fennel bulb fronds trimmed and reserved for another use (about 1-1/2 cups)
- 1 teaspoon olive oil for drizzling
- 1 tangerine, peeled and separated into sections, or substitute 1 orange or a handful of kumquats
- 2–3 cups fresh tender greens such as spinach or arugula
- 2–3 cups assorted sprouts such as beet sprouts, clover sprouts, alfalfa sprouts, and sunflower shoots
- 2 tablespoons tahini, stirred well
- 2 tablespoons fresh orange juice
- 1 teaspoon sherry vinegar or other mild vinegar
- 3 tablespoons walnuts toasted
- 3 tablespoons pomegranate seeds optional
- sea salt and fresh ground pepper to finish

Instructions

- Chop beetroots off from the greens. Save the beet greens for later—they're related to chard, are tender and mild-flavored, and terrific to add to soups, whole grain and bean dishes. It's free nourishment and less food waste.
- Rinse the whole beet and wrap tightly in foil. Place on baking sheet and roast for 1 hour. Chop the fennel bulb into bite-sized pieces. Spread on a rimmed baking sheet. Drizzle lightly with olive oil.
- Roast the fennel for 20 minutes stirring occasionally, so fennel is tender and golden. Remove from oven and allow to cool.
- Remove beets from oven and set aside. Once they're cool enough to handle, remove foil and rub the beets. Their skin should slip right off.
- Both beet and fennel may be roasted a day ahead, stored in airtight containers and chilled in the refrigerator.
- For the dressing, mix together the tahini and orange juice, stirring well to create a smooth, creamy dressing. Add that splash of vinegar and give a final stir.
- To assemble, channel your inner artist. Spread spinach or other tender greens on a platter or large, shallow bowl. Scatter on fennel.
- Sprinkle on assorted bean and green sprouts, then top with tangerine, beets, walnuts and pomegranate seeds, if adding.
- Finish with a sprinkle of sea salt and pepper. Dot dressing on top.
- Serves 4 to 6.

Miami Flavors—Collard Confetti

My Portuguese is pretty much limited to obrigata (thank you) and couve a miniera, Brazil's salad of shredded collards. Its simplicity invites a million spins. It's raw, can be made in minutes with a few pantry staples, but it's another case where less equals more.

How to serve: Collard confetti isn't meant to be a solo act. It's a traditional topping for feijoada (p. 85) and it makes a bright, green component for sancocho (p. 101), picadillo (p. 80), Cuban black beans (p. 88) or almost anything beany. Recipe doubles easily, and since collards are sturdy, make more for a party. It's confetti after all.

Ingredients

- 1/2 pound collard greens
- 1 garlic clove minced
- 1 tablespoon olive oil
- 2 tablespoons freshly squeezed lemon juice from 1 juicy lemon
- sea salt and fresh ground pepper to taste

Instructions

- Wash the collards well. Blot dry. Slice out their thick central stems and discard (or reserve them to make broth later). Stack the collard leaves and roll them up widthwise, forming a tight collard cigar. Using your sharpest knife, slice across as thinly as possible, forming skinny ribbons—collard confetti—or to use the proper culinary term, chiffonade.
- Alternately, shred the collards in a food processor, using the shredding disc. You'll have roughly 2 cups of greens.
- Scoop the collards into a large bowl. Add the minced garlic, lemon juice and olive oil. Toss to combine. Collards should have a nice glisten of oil but stay fresh and not soggy. Season with sea salt and pepper.
- Serves 4.

Miami Flavors—Tropical Slaw

Cole slaw has a million spins. This one has some Caribbean sass and sway and no mayonnaise. Frilly Napa cabbage is pretty in this, but your basic sturdy cabbage, green or purple, works too. Swapping chopped cashews for the almonds is also fine. The island accent and golden glow comes from the dressing of lime juice, coconut oil and mild turmeric-forward curry powder.

How to serve: This is a great slaw for a buffet or backyard barbecue, since it can sit out for a while without wilting or going nasty on you. Nice with Caribbean pigeon peas and rice (p. 92), tacu tacu (p. 90) or as part of a mix plate with papas asada (p. 126) and cowboy caviar (p. 136).

Ingredients

- 3 cups Napa cabbage, a good-sized wedge, shredded and loosely packed
- 1 red pepper (1 cup), shredded
- 2 carrots (1 cup), shredded
- 1 cup jicama, shredded
- 1 tablespoon coconut oil
- 1/4 cup lime juice
- 2 teaspoons Jamaican curry powder or other mild curry powder
- 1 teaspoon coconut sugar or agave
- sea salt and fresh ground pepper
- 1/4 cup toasted almonds, coarsely chopped
- handful of cilantro leaves

Instructions

- Use a food processor's shredder blade or work your knife skills and chop vegetables fine by hand. The end result should look like multicolored confetti.
- Tumble the shredded vegetables into a large bowl. Give them a taste of sea salt and fresh ground pepper, and toss to combine.
- For the dressing: gently heat coconut oil in a small pot over low heat on the stovetop or pop in the microwave for a second or two. Coconut oil is a saturated fat like butter. It solidifies when cold. You don't want it doing that when it meets the vegetables in this slaw. Now whisk in the lime juice, curry powder, and coconut sugar or agave until smooth and emulsified. Dressing will be thickish. There's just enough to hug the slaw.
- Spoon dressing over the shredded vegetables and toss everything together. Taste and add more sea salt and fresh ground pepper to taste. Finish with the chopped toasted almonds and cilantro leaves.
- Serves 4. Doubles or triples easily.

Miami Flavors—Miami Vegan Lettuce Cups with Heart

Lettuce cups spark up your appetite without heating up your kitchen, plus they're a great way to get kids—and grownups—to eat vegetables. This no-cook recipe reflects Miami's Asian influence, by way of Trinidad and Jamaica. Both have sizable Chinese communities that go back to the late 1800s. Avocado, hearts of palm, and orange–ginger dressing keep it tropical.

How to serve: This is most fun as a DIY affair, so let everyone make their own. Set out a plate of lettuce, a bowl of the hearts of palm filling, a bowl of the chopped herbs, and ramekins with extras including:

- chopped roasted peanuts or cashews
- toasted sesame seeds
- sriracha and mayo dipping sauce
- chili crisp
- extra orange-ginger dressing/dipping sauce

Take a generous-sized tender leaf, sprinkle on a few of the assorted chopped herbs, then top with the hearts of palm salad. Spoon on any desired garnishes. Fold the lettuce ends toward the middle, so you have a nice lettuce package.

If you've had a particularly hectic day, bypass the wraps and just eat the hearts of palm mixture as a chopped salad. It's really good.

Feel free to swap out the vegetables in the filling. Possible substitutes include:

- 1/2 cup cucumber, diced
- 1/2 cup red pepper, chopped
- 1-2 carrots, chopped into matchsticks
- 1/2 cup cabbage, shredded

Hold on to the avocado and hearts of palm, though. That's what makes it Miami.

Ingredients

For the dressing/dipping sauce:

- 1/4 cup fresh orange juice
- 2 tablespoons soy sauce or tamari
- 1 tablespoon sesame oil
- 1 teaspoon fresh ginger, minced
- 1 teaspoon evaporated cane sugar or palm sugar

For the lettuce cups:

- 1-1/2 cups fresh bean sprouts
- 1-1/2 cups organic hearts of palm (1 15-ounce can hearts of palm, drained), chopped
- 1/2 cup radish, daikon or jicama, chopped into matchsticks
- 4 ounces firm tofu, diced
- 1/2 Florida avocado or 1 whole Hass avocado (1 cup)), diced
- sea salt and fresh ground pepper to taste
- 1 handful fresh mint leaves, chopped
- 1 handful fresh cilantro, chopped
- 1 handful fresh Thai basil or other basil, chopped
- 1 handful scallions, sliced thin
- 1 head Boston, butter, or other tender lettuce, hydroponic or traditionally grown

Instructions

- In a small bowl, whisk together the fresh orange juice, soy sauce, sesame oil, minced ginger and cane sugar until sugar dissolves and the dressing is combined. Set aside.
- In a large bowl, mix together bean sprouts, hearts of palm, the chopped radish or jicama, and the firm tofu. Add the avocado and pour in about half the orange–ginger dressing. Season with sea salt and pepper and stir together gently, so the avocado stays intact.
- Just before serving, combine all the chopped mint, cilantro, basil and scallions in a separate bowl.
- Tear or slice away the lettuce leaves at the base, and set them out on a plate for the lettuce cups.
- Serves 4.

Ceviche

If ever a dish was made for Miami, this is the one. Ceviche is a cool and refreshing no-cook classic, citrus-infused and chili-spiked, all the things we love. Ecuador, Peru, and Polynesia all lay claim to inventing ceviche, and there are versions all over the globe. One problem—the traditional star of ceviche is seafood. The fish is über-fresh and the acid in the citrus serves to cook it—cure it, really, breaking down the fibers and creating tenderness. Genius technique, but not vegan. The thing is, ceviche isn' t really about the fish. It's about the flavor, the texture, the temperature, the zing. That's all accomplished by leche de tigre—means tiger milk, but it's the tiger-free secret sauce that bathes your main ingredient, which should be firm in texture but mild in flavor, something the citrus will kiss and cure and the chile will befriend.

We're keeping with ceviche's multiple varieties but freeing the fish. Can't decide between mushroom, papaya/tofu or hearts of palm with grapefruit and avocado? Make them all and have a party.

How to serve: Ceviche is a terrific summer starter, great for a party or buffet, since it's best made ahead and allowed to marinate. Its bright colors make any day a celebration. Serve in oversized porcelain Asian soup spoons to enjoy in a single slurp. Serve in martini glasses for more generous appetizer portions. Set out extra bowls of diced onion, chopped cilantro, lime quarters, diced avocado, and thinly sliced jalapeño, and let guests help themselves.

Ceviche is traditionally served with plantain chips or popcorn. Yes, really.

Miami Favorites—Papaya-Tofu Ceviche

A citrus-chile bath gives ripe papaya the look and texture of raw fish. It gives tofu the glam treatment it deserves. I've made this recipe with just papaya and again with just tofu. They're better together.

Ingredients

- 1/3 cup fresh lemon juice
- 1/3 cup fresh lime juice
- 1/3 cup fresh orange juice
- 1 jalapeño or 1/2 teaspoon Scotch bonnet pepper, seeded and chopped fine
- 1 medium onion (about 1 cup), chopped fine
- 1-2 red pepper (about 1 cup), chopped fine
- 3 ripe plum tomatoes, chopped or half a pint of grape tomatoes, sliced
- 8 ounces ripe papaya, cut into bite-sized cubes
- 8 ounces extra-firm tofu (half a 1-pound package), preferably organic, pressed to expel excess water and sliced into bite-sized cubes
- 1 bunch of cilantro, chopped fine, plus more for garnish, if desired
- 1 bunch Italian parsley, chopped fine
- 1 dozen radishes (about 1 cup), sliced thin or 1 cup jicama, diced
- sea salt to taste
- 1 ripe Florida avocado, chopped or sliced thin

Instructions

- Pour lemon, lime, and orange juice into a large bowl. Add chopped onion, red pepper and jalapeño or Scotch bonnet and chopped tomatoes. Stir together well. Add papaya and tofu and season generously with sea salt. Mix together lightly, so as not to mush the tofu.
- Cover tightly and refrigerate for at least 2 hours. To serve, taste again. Don't be afraid to add more sea salt. Gently stir in chopped cilantro, and top with scattered diced radish or jicama and chopped or sliced avocado.
- Serves 6 to 8.

Miami Favorites—Mushroom Ceviche

Giving mushrooms a quick steam before their citrus-chile marinade bath deepens their flavor and makes them more digestible.

Ingredients

- 8 ounces cremini or white button mushrooms, sliced
- 1 sheet nori
- 1 pepper—green, yellow, orange, red, your choice, diced (about 1-1/2 cups)
- 1/2 jalapeño, minced
- 3 tablespoons red or purple onion, diced
- 1 small tomato, chopped (about 1/4 cup)
- 1/3 cup fresh lime juice
- sea salt to taste
- big handful of cilantro leaves, chopped

Instructions

- Tumble sliced mushrooms into the top of a double-boiler or steamer. Add the nori sheet.
- Cover and steam for 5 minutes, just until the mushrooms darken and begin to turn juicy. The mushrooms will have picked up a little briny flavor from the nori. Discard nori sheet.
- Pour the mushrooms in a large glass or ceramic bowl. Add diced pepper, minced jalapeño, diced onion, chopped tomato, and lime juice.
- Give everything a good mix, and a little pinch of sea salt. Cover and refrigerate for at least 4 hours or overnight.
- Just before serving, add chopped cilantro, taste again for salt, toss and serve.
- Serves 4.

Miami Favorites—Hearts of Palm Ceviche with Grapefruit and Avocado

The simplest of the three ceviches is the most Miami. Grapefruit gets a chance to shine here, adding a juicy burst of brightness and a whisper of floral notes. Grapefruit's botanical name is citrus paradisi, so enjoy a taste of paradise.

Avocado softens any grapefruit acidity, and adds some luscious, sexy, heart-healthy fat. The third tropical element, hearts of palm, was once so plentiful in South Florida, folks called it swamp cabbage. It now needs to be grown, harvested, and sourced with care. Cutting out the heart, the tender center of the palm not only kills the tree, it can damage an entire ecosystem like the Amazonian rainforest or the Florida Everglades. But there's a sustainable solution. Some palm species (and there's over 2,500) are multi-stemmed, so the tree lives after the heart of one trunk is harvested. Choosing canned sustainable and/or organic hearts of palm means there'll be hearts of palm for everyone now and for years and vegan ceviches to come.

Ingredients

- 1–15-ounce can organic hearts of palm, drained, long stems sliced into squidlike rings
- 1 cup fresh grapefruit, (about half a grapefruit), chopped + 1/4 cup fresh grapefruit juice
- 1/2 jalapeño, minced
- 2 tablespoons purple onion, minced
- 1 cup avocado (about half a Florida avocado or 1 Hass), diced
- a handful of cilantro leaves, chopped

Instructions

- Pour drained hearts of palm into a glass or ceramic bowl. Add chopped grapefruit and grapefruit juice, the minced jalapeño, and minced onion. Give everything a good stir. Then cover and chill for at least 30 minutes.
- Just before serving, add diced avocado and chopped cilantro.
- Serves 4.

Sizzles, Hot Pots, and Potcakes—Miami Mains

Miami Favorites—Haitian Bean Gravy—Sos Pwa

Say sauce. Say pwa (or pois, if you want to be French about it). Sos pwa, meaning pea sauce, is Haitian comfort food, and one of those genius dishes that give you more for less. Some families make sos pwa as a soup, others make a thicker, saucier sos, like this one. Simple to make, luscious to eat.

How to serve: Traditionally, this velvety, satisfying sauce is served over rice or mais moulen, which means cornmeal mush. Which basically means sofkee (p. 132). It's also nice paired with a good-sized wedge of cornbread (p. 34) or a few hoecakes right from the skillet (p. 32). Adding a splash of hot sauce is a good idea.

Ingredients

- 1 tablespoon olive oil
- 1 small onion chopped (about 1 cup)
- 2 garlic cloves chopped
- 2 scallions chopped, plus additional for garnish, if desired
- 1 sprig fresh thyme leaves plus additional for garnish, if desired
- 1 15-ounce can red beans rinsed and drained or 2 cups cooked red beans
- 2/3 cup reserved bean cooking liquid or vegetable broth
- 1/2 cup full-fat coconut milk
- sea salt and fresh ground pepper to taste.

Instructions

- Heat olive oil in a saucepan over medium-high heat. Add the chopped onion, garlic and scallions and sauté, stirring occasionally until the vegetables become tender, burnished and fragrant, about 8 minutes. Add the thyme, and the beans, and bean cooking liquid or vegetable broth.
- Purée the beans until they're very smooth, using an immersion blender (or transfer to a food processor or blender), for 3–5 minutes. For extra smoothness, strain the mixture through a sieve.
- Return the beans to the saucepan. Swirl in the coconut milk. Heat through and reduce over medium heat for about 10 minutes, until the flavors meld and the bean sauce thickens enough to coat the back of a spoon.
- Season generously with sea salt and fresh ground pepper. Finish with a scattering of extra thyme leaves and snipped scallions if you like.
- Serves 4.

Miami Favorites—Bahamian Chowder

Bahamians were among Miami's first solid communities, settling in Coconut Grove in the 19th century, bringing with them their own foodways, including conch (pronounced conk). Its elegant conical shell distracts from the fact that conch is a large sea snail with tough flesh that requires marinating, tenderizing, pounding and grinding—such violence!—before making its way into two South Florida favorites—conch fritters and conch chowder.

This chowder saves the conch and saves you a lot of effort. Nori dust* provides conch's briny flavor, and minced firm tofu mimics its chewy texture.

Bahamian chowder is tomato-rich and brothy like Manhattan clam chowder, but it doesn't have city chic. Or clams. Still, it contains nori, the same thing used to wrap sushi—so it qualifies as seafood.

A big bowl of Bahamian chowder is just the thing after a day out on the water, when you're happy, tired, and lacquered with sea salt, sunscreen, and sweat. It's also good after a crappy workday. Ladle up a bowl, put on some goombay, and imagine running away to the Bahamas.

How to serve: Serve with a good-sized wedge of cornbread (p. 34) fresh from the oven, and set a bottle of hot sauce on the table.

Ingredients

- 3 tablespoons olive oil
- 1 large onion, well-chopped (about 1-1/2 cup)
- 4 garlic cloves, minced
- 1 sliver Scotch bonnet or 1/2 jalapeño, minced
- 3–4 celery stalks, well-chopped (about 2 cups)
- 2 carrots, well-chopped (about 1 cup)
- 1-2 red peppers, well-chopped (about 1 cup)
- 1 small fennel bulb (about 1 cup), well-chopped
- 1/2 pound potatoes (about 2 cups), well-chopped
- 1 14-ounce can chopped tomatoes or 2 cups ripe, fresh tomatoes, chopped
- 5 cups vegetable broth
- 1 tablespoon tomato paste
- 1/2 cup white wine*
- 1 teaspoon thyme
- 1 teaspoon allspice

---

* Available in Asian markets, many grocery stores, and online.

- 2 teaspoons Old Bay seasoning
- 1 bay leaf
- 1 teaspoon nori dust**
- 1 cup firm tofu, pressed to expel any extra water, minced (about half a 1 pound package)
- sea salt and fresh ground pepper to taste

Instructions

- In a large soup pot, heat olive oil over medium–high heat. When it starts to shimmer, add chopped onions and minced garlic. Cook, stirring for a minute, then add the Scotch bonnet or jalapeño, celery, carrots, red pepper, fennel, and potatoes and continue cooking and stirring until vegetables start to soften, another 10 minutes.
- Spoon in tomato paste, pour in the wine, chopped tomatoes, and broth. Stir and scrape any vegetable bits stuck to the bottom of the pot. Add the allspice, Old Bay, and bay leaf. Continue stirring and bring the mixture to a boil.
- Cover, reduce heat to low, and allow chowder to simmer for 45 minutes or until potatoes are tender and flavors have melded. Finish by stirring in nori dust, sea salt, and fresh ground pepper.
- Serves 6. Doubles well.

** Feel free to omit wine and substitute an additional ½ cup vegetable broth.

Mushrooms

Mushrooms thrive in the cold, damp, and dark. So how can they grow in Miami? Indoors. In warehouse space and shipping containers, retrofitted so they're specially climate and light controlled. At least three local farms—Paradise Farms, SOL Mushrooms, and Gratitude Gardens—have been cultivating exotic in-demand varietals like lion's mane, maitake and oyster mushrooms. This is a wonderful thing.

Not so long ago, you had to be a chef (or rich) to get your hands on them, but local cultivation has put culinary mushrooms within reach for the rest of us. Rich, savory, chewy, and umami, mushrooms earn their place in the kitchen and in the clinic. They've been used in Traditional Chinese Medicine and Ayurvedic healing for centuries. They're fiber-rich and high in potassium, selenium, and vitamin D, all linked to boosting your mood. Paradise and gratitude, indeed.

We all deserve access to paradise. But white button mushrooms work fine in these recipes.

Miami Favorites—Djon Djon Rice

Djon djon are mushrooms growing wild in the north of Haiti. They're black, intensely earthy, and usually dried after harvest to preserve them. Haitians cook the dried djon djon with rice for a dish that's far more than its simple parts. Dried djon djon are soaked in hot water, which releases their flavor and color, and then the rice is cooked in the mushroom broth. Djon djon rice has the luscious texture of a risotto, but is easier to make. There's not a lot of stirring, it cooks pretty much on its own, and the taste is a wow. The umami is right there in the mushrooms So is the blackness. The blacker the rice, the more it's djon djon-infused, and the more it's prized. Dried djon djon are available in a good many Miami markets but perhaps not where you are. Don't fret, any dried mushroom will do. It may not cook up as black, but it'll still be delicious.

However, if the idea of black rice gives you a charge, try making this dish using forbidden black rice. Yes, it's a bit of a cheat that way, but forbidden black rice is nutty, heady and delicious. You can also swap out rice for another whole grain like farro, which has about the same cooking time as rice.

How to serve: Djon djon is often served as a party dish. It's a party in the mouth for sure and can be doubled to serve a crowd. Even better, it can be made a day ahead, and the flavors deepen and develop. It pairs beautifully with a salad, the prettier the better, like Miami Beet Salad (p. 56) or a nice array of roasted vegetables. A jar of pikliz (p. 122) wouldn't be out of place, either.

Ingredients

- 1 cup brown rice or black rice
- 1/2 cup dried mushrooms—djon djon, if available, but any dried mushrooms will do
- 1 small onion, chopped fine (about 1/2 cup)
- 2 garlic cloves, minced
- 3 tablespoons olive oil
- 8 ounces fresh mushrooms, chopped—white button mushrooms or more exotic varieties like shiitakes, oyster mushrooms, and others
- fresh thyme leaves from one or two good-sized sprigs, if available
- sliver of Scotch bonnet or 1/2 jalapeño, minced
- sea salt and fresh ground pepper to taste

Instructions

- Pour dried mushrooms into a large bowl. Bring 3 cups of water to boil. Pour the hot water over the mushrooms. When the hot water meets the dried mushrooms, the mushrooms reconstitute and the hot water becomes mushroom broth—magic! Kinda.
- Pour rice into a bowl. Cover with cold water.
- Leave the mushrooms to reconstitute and infuse the hot water and the rice to soften for 2 hours, longer if possible.
- Strain the mushrooms and any grit and reserve the broth. In many Haiti kitchens, the djon djon are discarded at this point. I can't let a mushroom go. Give the mushrooms a fine chop.
- Heat the oil in a large saucepan over medium-high heat. Once it starts to shimmer, add the chopped onion.

- Sauté and stir for 3 minutes or so, until onion turns golden and softens. Add minced garlic and the chopped reconstituted dried mushrooms and Scotch bonnet or jalapeño. Stir well to incorporate, allowing vegetables to cook and soften.
- Add the chopped fresh mushrooms and give a stir. Dense shiitakes will take 8–10 minutes, while soft, tender oyster mushrooms cook in just a few minutes. In either case, once cooked, they'll release a little more liquid. This is good.
- Drain and rinse the rice and add it to the pot. Stir to coat, so grains are gilded with oil. Turn up the heat to high and pour in reserved mushroom broth. Bring everything to a boil. Reduce heat to low and cover,
- Let the rice cook for 30 minutes or until the grains are plump and have absorbed all the mushroom broth. Add thyme leaves and season generously with sea salt and freshly ground pepper. Give everything a good stir.
- Replace the lid, take the pot off the burner, and allow the rice to rest for about 10 minutes. Then serve and enjoy.
- Serves 4.

Miami Flavors—Mushroom Étouffée

Étouffée, a classic Creole dish, takes its name from the French verb étouffer—to asphyxiate or smother. Doesn't sound fun. But smothering, a beloved technique in traditional Southern cooking, makes for a party in the mouth. Vegetables are browned, dusted with flour and spices, then doused with broth and wine, creating a rich gravy. It's a party for the cook, too, with all the action taking place in one pot.

Exotic mushrooms such as maitake are spectacular here, but even white button mushrooms blossom when given the étouffée treatment.

How to serve. Over rice. White rice is the New Orleans standard, but brown rice offers mild nutty flavor and a little whole grain goodness. Also great ladled over sofkee (p. 132), better known here as grits.

Ingredients

- 3 tablespoons vegan butter
- 1 large onion, chopped (about 1-1/2 cups)
- 2 stalks celery, chopped (about 1-1/2 cups)
- 1/2 red, orange, or yellow or other sweet pepper, chopped (about 1/2 cup)
- 3 cloves garlic, minced
- 1/2 jalapeño, minced
- 2 tablespoons unbleached all-purpose flour
- 1/3 cup red wine*
- 1 cup chopped tomatoes
- 1/2 cup vegetable broth
- 2 teaspoons Creole or blackened seasoning (or substitute 1 teaspoon each paprika and garlic, plus a pinch of cayenne)
- 1 bay leaf
- 8 ounces mushrooms, chopped
- sprig of fresh thyme
- sea salt and fresh ground pepper

---

* If you wish to do without the wine, add additional vegetable broth.

Instructions

- In a Dutch oven or soup pot, melt vegan butter over medium-high heat. When it starts to foam, add the chopped onion, chopped celery, and chopped sweet pepper. Cook, stirring, for 3 to 5 minutes or until vegetables begin to soften and turn golden.ss
- Add the minced garlic and jalapeño. Give a stir and cook until the vegetables begin to relax and turn fragrant.
- Sprinkle the unbleached flour over all—no need to sift—and continue stirring until vegetables are coated. Cook for another few minutes, until the flour absorbs all the vegetable juices and starts to toast.
- Add chopped tomatoes, wine, and broth.
- Stir to combine and continue cooking until the mixture comes together and forms a thick sauce. Add Creole seasoning and bay leaf. Keep stirring, reducing heat to medium, should the etouffée start to stick to the bottom of the pot.
- Tumble in the chopped mushrooms and gently stir to combine. It may appear there's not enough sauce to coat the mushrooms, but continue cooking for another 5–10 minutes. The mushrooms break down and soften under heat, producing their own rich broth.
- Stir so everything incorporates. Mushrooms and other vegetables should be tender, not mushy, and the gravy should be about the consistency of heavy cream—not gluey, not soupy. Add the leaves from a sprig of thyme, then season generously with sea salt and freshly ground pepper.
- Serves 4 to 6.

Latin Influence

Everybody knows about the Miami–Cuba connection—we're only 90 miles apart. But our Latin influence extends far beyond Cuban culture. We have communities from Nicaragua, Venezuela, Colombia, Mexico, Brazil, the Dominican Republic, Honduras, Guatemala, Puerto Rico, and I'm probably forgetting some (sorry). The Spanish, though, got here first.

The Spanish explorer Ponce de Leon washed up north of Miami in 1513. He was so besotted with our lush tropical foliage, he named the place Florida, for flowery. Then he claimed it for Spain—kind of nervy, really.

That original Spanish connection is still part of Miami. The Monastery Church of Saint Bernard de Clairvaux in North Miami Beach is Spanish, despite its French-sounding name, Believed to be the oldest building in the Western Hemisphere or at least the United States, it also goes by the accurate if not romantic name of the Ancient Spanish Monastery.

Built outside Segovia, it dates back to the 12th century where it housed a Cistercian order for some 700 years. Then came a revolution or two, and the monastery was closed. William Randolph Hearst purchased the church and its cloisters in 1924, had it dismantled brick by brick and had it shipped to the United States. Who knows why? It sat in crates for decades.

In the '60s, a wealthy Episcopal benefactor bought it as a gift for the Florida bishop. The bishop had it reassembled, the monastery was back in business, and has had an active Episcopal congregation ever since.

Sweeping Romanesque arches and elaborately wrought marble columns set the church and its cloisters apart from the rest of Miami, which prizes the new and the now. We hustle on past, oblivious, taken up with our busy, busy lives. The church, nestled outside the flow of traffic, doesn't mind. Like our connection to Spain, it's still here.

Miami Favorites—Arroz con Jaca o Soya—Cuban Rice and Jackfruit or Rice and Tempeh

No Cuban celebration or family or community gathering would be complete without arroz con pollo—chicken and rice, But it won't be vegan with a chicken, will it? Jackfruit stands in beautifully. So does house-smoked tempeh (p. 139) or extra-firm tofu.

Ingredients

- 1 pound fresh green jackfruit, or 20-ounce can young green jackfruit in brine, rinsed and drained or 1 pound house-smoked tempeh or 1 pound extra-firm tofu, sliced into strips
- 1 tablespoon olive oil
- 2 garlic cloves, minced
- 1/2 teaspoon cumin
- pinch turmeric
- sea salt and fresh ground pepper

For the rice

- 2 cups brown rice
- 2 tablespoons olive oil
- 1 large onion, diced (about 2 cups)
- 3 garlic cloves, minced
- 1 red pepper, diced (about 1 cup)
- 2 bay leaves
- 1 teaspoon dried oregano, crumbled or fresh culantro,* chopped
- 1 teaspoon cumin
- 1/2 teaspoon annatto or pinch saffron
- 1 teaspoon turmeric
- 1 teaspoon garlic powder
- 1 teaspoon onion powder
- 1/3 cup white wine
- 3 cups vegetable broth
- 2 cups chopped tomatoes or 1 15-ounce can chopped tomatoes

---

* Available online, at most Whole Foods, Sprouts, and Asian markets.

- 1 cup peas (frozen and thawed peas are fine)
- sea salt and fresh ground pepper

To finish:
- 1 tablespoon capers, rinsed and drained
- 1/2 cup green olives, chopped
- 1/2 cup pimento (jarred), sliced into strips

Instructions

- Soak brown rice in a bowl of cold water to cover. Set aside.
- In a separate good-size bowl, whisk together olive oil, minced garlic, cumin, and turmeric until combined.
- Pour in jackfruit, using a fork to break apart any large bits. Or add tempeh or tofu trips, if substituting. Stir to combine so everything gets a little coating of the spiced oil. Season generously with sea salt and pepper and set aside to marinate for 15–30 minutes while you get the sofrito going.
- In a large soup pot with a lid, heat olive oil over medium-high heat. Add onion and stir occasionally until onion softens and moves toward becoming golden, 5–7 minutes.
- Add the minced garlic and diced red pepper. Continue cooking and stirring until all the vegetables are softened and fragrant.
- Add the bay leaves, culantro or oregano, cumin, saffron, turmeric, garlic powder, and onion powder, and stir just for a minute or so, until you have a richly seasoned oil.
- Rinse the brown rice, drain well, and stir into the sofrito. Give the rice a good gloss from the oil. Then add the broth, wine, and chopped tomatoes.
- Let everything come to a boil, stirring occasionally, then cover and reduce heat to low. Cook for 15 minutes, until rice is still on the crunchy side but is starting to soften and gather flavor.
- Add the jackfruit or its soy-based stand-in and its marinade. Stir to combine, cover and continue cooking for another 15 minutes or so until the rice is tender and has soaked up all the broth, tomatoes, and wine.
- Stir in the peas just at the end, so they heat through but stay bright green. Gray peas don't cut it. Fish out the bay leaves and discard. Season generously with sea salt and pepper.
- To serve like a local, spoon rice into a deep casserole or baking dish. Smooth the top and arrange chopped olives, pimentos, and capers on top.
- Or just scatter in olives, pimentos and capers and dish up right out of the pot.
- Serves 6.

Miami Favorites—Picadillo

A staple dish at many of Miami's Latino eateries, picadillo is a sloppy joe with a Spanish accent. There are versions all over South and Central America, but at its heart, it's sautéed ground beef, made savory by simmering with tomatoes, olives, and capers and ever-so-slightly sweet with raisins. Sounds crazy, but it's crazy-good. Even crazier is my version, which substitutes lentils and chopped walnuts for the beef. They stay true to ground beef's texture, pretty much equal the protein, and up the fiber.

How to serve: Most Cuban restaurants serve this with white rice. I respectfully suggest brown, so you skip the simple carbs and amp up the savory flavors. You can also dollop a healthy serving of picadillo onto a bun for a hot handheld—not tidy but it can't taste anything but good.

I keep wanting to add chile heat to this dish, but Cuban cuisine doesn't skew spicy. I'm breaking with tradition enough by messing with the recipe. I live here, I don't want to piss off my neighbors more than I have to. If you want to hot it up, splash on some hot sauce when you serve. Or spoon up some pikliz (p. 122) on your plate.

Ingredients

- 3 cups brown lentils, cooked and cooled (from 1-1/2 cups dried lentils)
- 1 cup walnuts, chopped
- 2 tablespoon olive oil
- 1 onion, chopped (about 1-1/2 cups)
- 3 garlic cloves, minced
- 1 red pepper, chopped (about 1 cup)
- 2 tomatoes, chopped or 1 15-ounce can chopped tomato
- 1 teaspoon cumin
- 1 teaspoon dried oregano
- 1 teaspoon smoked paprika
- 1/3 cup pitted green olives, chopped
- 1/3 cup raisins
- 1 tablespoon capers. rinsed and drained
- sea salt and fresh ground pepper to taste

Instructions

- In a large skillet, heat oil over medium-high heat. When it starts to shimmer, add chopped onion, minced garlic, and chopped red pepper. Cook, stirring occasionally, until vegetables soften and become slightly golden and fragrant, about 8 minutes.
- Stir in the tomato, cumin, oregano, and smoked paprika. Add the cooked lentils, walnuts, chopped olives, raisins, and capers, taking care not to smoosh the lentils.
- Cover and reduce heat to low. Cook for another 10 minutes or until heated through. Season with sea salt and fresh ground pepper.
- Serves 4. Doubles easily for a party.

Miami Flavors—Chickpeas with Saffron

This is a vegan riff on the Catalan classic fabada Asturiana (pork and bean stew). There's no pork here, but plenty of beans and plenty of rich flavor. A sofrito (easy sauté) of tomato, onions, garlic, and spices builds flavor and replaces the animal products. The addition of saffron is traditional and brilliant, adding an earthy richness.

While usually made with white beans, I like it with chickpeas with their more assertive flavor. But if you've got white beans, honey, use 'em. Use canned beans if you must—you'll need 6 cups or 3 15-ounce cans of beans. I'm telling you, though, cooking up dried beans results in a truly sumptuous and satisfying dish. The beans are more tender than canned and absorb all the spices and aromatics.

This is one of those low and slow-cooking dishes. You could fast-forward by using an Instant pot.

How to serve: In Spain, this can be served as part of a tapas spread. I like it as a main course. It's gutsy and luxe—that's the beauty of beans. Serve with crusty whole grain bread, roasted vegetables or a green salad. It's a total meant-to-be with Catalan spinach (p. 55).

Ingredients

- 1 pound dried chickpeas rinsed, picked over and soaked overnight with cold water to cover, plus a pinch of baking soda or 3 15-ounce cans chickpeas or white beans, rinsed and drained

For the sofrito:

- 3 tablespoons olive oil
- 1 onion, chopped (about 1 cup)
- 4 cloves garlic, minced
- 2 large ripe tomatoes, peeled and chopped or 1 15-ounce can chopped tomatoes, preferably fire-roasted
- 1 tablespoon liquid smoke
- 1 tablespoon smoked paprika
- 1 generous pinch saffron threads
- sea salt and fresh ground pepper to taste
- a handful cilantro, chopped, if desired

Instructions

- Bring 6 cups of water to boil in a large soup pot. Pour in the beans, drop in the garlic, add the bay leaf and pepper flakes, if using. Give the pot a hard boil on high heat for 10 minutes, then cover and reduce the heat to low. Let beans simmer, covered for an hour, or until they're just tender, not mushy.
- If you're using canned beans, start here, with the sofrito.
- In a large pot, heat the olive oil over medium-high heat, for about 3 minutes or until shimmering. Add the chopped onion and minced garlic. Sauté the vegetables for about 5–8 minutes or until they soften and smell fragrant. Reduce heat to medium and pour in the chopped tomatoes. Add the liquid smoke and smoked paprika, crumble in the saffron threads, and add it to the tomatoes. Stir together.
- Continue cooking and stirring for about 8–10 minutes or until the sauce starts to thicken and darken to a deep brick color.
- Remove the lid from the bean pot. The beans should have soaked up most but not all the water. Pour in the sofrito and stir to combine. Let the beans continue to cook, uncovered, for another 45 minutes, stirring occasionally or until the sauce reduces and coats the beans.
- Remove from heat and let cool. Season generously with sea salt and freshly ground pepper. Garnish with the fresh, chopped cilantro leaves, if using.
- Serves 6 to 8.

 # Rice and Beans

Miami sparkles with Michelin stars, restaurants where if you want a table tonight, you should have reserved last month, and chefs on whom I have culinary crushes. However, if you really want to get me excited, fix me rice and beans. They connect us.

Miami is home to a delicious mix of Latin and Caribbean communities—Cubans, Haitians, Dominicans, Trinis, Puerto Ricans, Jamaicans, Guatemalans, Venezuelans, Colombians, Brazilians, Costa Ricans, Nicaraguans, and more. Every one of them has their own rice and bean recipe that's not just delicious, it's the taste of home.

Your rice and beans will be different from my rice and beans. That's part of their beauty. Beans and rice happily soak up the flavors they're cooked with. But at core, they all offer belly-filling comfort and budget-stretching nourishment. They're affordable, digestible, accessible, versatile, satisfying, soulful, and culturally appropriate for every culture. In every language and every kind of cookery. a plate of beans and rice says, there, there, dear, it's going to be all right.

Miami Favorites—Feijoada

Dried beans have been called the poor man's meat. This sounds like a diss, but I think it's a plus. They offer a satisfying, meaty texture without the meat, are easy on the wallet, and they're the soul of this stew. It's called feijoada, and it's Brazil's national dish. Beans get top billing (the Portuguese word for beans is feijão) but feijoada is traditionally made with a whole lotta pork, too—bacon, salt pork, sausage, and pork ribs. Not here it isn't.

Without the pork, what saves this feijoada from being just another pot of black beans? Another traditional ingredient—orange. Black beans and orange love each other. Earthy, chocolaty, and chewy, black beans come together with dazzling orange in a way that muscles out any need for meat.

The splash of cider vinegar at the end may sound odd, but don't skip it. It adds balance and a little etching of acidity. It gives feijoada the hi def treatment. Despite the vinegar, feijoada is not sharp, and it's not spicy. It's rich and umami. To have a pot simmering on the stove is to feel rich indeed.

How to serve: Serve feijoada the way it deserves, with rice. White rice is traditional but you know me by now, brown rice offers extra whole grain goodness, and besides, I've already flouted convention by skipping the many meats. Serve with little bowls of sliced oranges, chopped onion, collard confetti (p. 57), and hot sauce. A big, bold Rioja wouldn't be out of place here either.

As with sancocho (p. 101), Caribbean curry (p. 112), Cuban black beans (p. 88), and so many of the other slow-cooking hot pots I love, feijoada's flavors get richer and more complex a day or two after you make it. Enjoy it today, enjoy it even more tomorrow. I understand feijoada freezes well. I've never had enough leftovers to try it.

Ingredients

For the beans:
- 1 pound dried black beans, rinsed and picked over
- 1 large onion, peeled and halved
- 1 orange, halved
- 6 garlic cloves
- 1 bay leaf
- 1 sliver Scotch bonnet pepper or pinch red pepper flakes
- 1/4 teaspoon dried oregano or a sprig or two of fresh oregano
- 1 teaspoon cumin

For the sofrito:
- 2 tablespoons olive oil
- 1 large onion, chopped (about 1-1/2 cups)

- 4 cloves garlic, minced
- 1 red pepper, chopped (about 1 cup)
- 1 sliver Scotch bonnet pepper, 1/2 jalapeño, minced, or pinch red pepper flakes
- 1 teaspoon annatto (optional)
- 2 teaspoons smoked paprika
- 2 tablespoons tomato paste
- zest of 1 orange
- 1 teaspoon apple cider vinegar
- sea salt and fresh ground pepper

Instructions

- Drain black beans and tip them into a large soup pot. Cover with about an inch of water. Drop in the onion, orange, garlic cloves, bay leaf, oregano, cumin, and Scotch bonnet or red pepper flakes.
- Bring to a boil over high heat and continue boiling for 10 minutes. Then reduce heat to low, cover the pot, and let the beans cook for about an hour or until the beans have soaked up most of the water and are just shy of being tender and done. Most of the orange will have melted into the feijoada, but press any orange flesh that remains into the bean mixture, then discard the orange rind, and the bay leaf.
- This is Feijoada Phase One. If you've had a busy day, you can allow the beans and their broth to cool, then pour into a large airtight container and refrigerate overnight before continuing. But if you're feeling the feijoada, move straight on to Feijoada Phase Two: the sofrito.
- Make the sofrito. In a large soup pot, heat oil over medium-high heat. Add the chopped onions, cook for a few minutes, giving them an occasional stir, until they soften and turn golden. Reduce heat to medium and add the minced garlic, chopped pepper, and Scotch bonnet or red pepper flakes. Continue cooking, stirring occasionally, for another 8–10 minutes, so the vegetables soften and turn fragrant and glisten with olive oil. Add all the black beans and about 2 cups of their own inky bean broth. Reserve any additional broth. Gently stir the beans into the sofrito.
- Add the annatto, if using, along with the smoked paprika, tomato paste, and orange zest. Give feijoada another stir or two,
- When it starts to bubble, reduce heat to low, cover, and let the stew simmer for 30–45 minutes, so flavors meld and become friendly. If feijoada is too dry for your liking, add the reserved bean broth, 1/2 cup at a time until you achieve flawless feijoada.
- Add the cider vinegar and season generously with sea salt and freshly ground pepper.
- Serves 6 to 8.

Miami Favorites—Cuban Black Beans

In Cuban restaurants, black beans often come as a pork accompaniment or afterthought. They deserve center stage. Cuban black beans have a smokiness and richness all their own, thanks to a slow-cooking sofrito. The only tinkering with tradition here is my addition of greens. Totally optional, but hey, they're sustainable, nutrient-dense, and anti-aging.

How to serve: Cuban eateries traditionally serve black beans as a side dish with white rice and sautéed plantains. I like black beans as a main attraction, with a big green salad. Go wild and keep the plantains (p. 143), and swap out the rice for hoecakes (p. 32) or grits cakes (p. 134).

Ingredients

- 3 tablespoons olive oil
- 2 onions, chopped (about 2-1/2 cups)
- 4 garlic cloves, chopped
- 1 red pepper, chopped (about 1 cup)
- 1 jalapeño or other hot chile, chopped
- 1 pound dried black beans, cooked and cooled
- 2 tablespoons tomato paste
- 1 tablespoon smoked paprika
- 2 teaspoons cumin
- 2 tablespoons sherry vinegar or 1 tablespoon cider vinegar
- 1/2 pound kale or Swiss chard, sliced into skinny ribbons (aka chiffonade), about 2 cups
- sea salt and fresh ground pepper to taste

Instructions

- In a large soup pot, heat olive oil over medium-high heat. Add onions and cook, stirring, until they start to sweat, about 5 minutes. Add garlic and both the sweet and hot pepper.
- Stir to combine and reduce heat to medium. Cook the vegetables, stirring occasionally, for another 15 minutes, until they're softened and aromatic. Add cumin, tomato paste, and smoked paprika, and stir until combined, and vegetables have taken on a warm and rosy glow.
- Stir in the black beans and about 1 cup of the bean cooking broth. Reduce heat to medium, and set the pot lid on halfway, leaving a little steam vent. Cook the beans for an hour, longer if you've got the time. Add more bean broth, 1/2 cup at a time, if the beans seem dry. Aim for thick, not over-dry. The goal is a divine beanly sludge.
- Stir in the sherry or cider vinegar. Remove from heat.
- Add the chiffonade of kale or chard by the handful. Stir gently, letting the greens wilt into the beans.
- Season generously with sea salt and ground pepper.
- Serves 6 to 8.

Miami Flavors—Tacu Tacu

Tacu tacu—fun name, and a genius Peruvian makeover for rice and beans. It's not a stew, it's a skillet dish, a potcake, crusty and comforting. Traditionally, tacu tacu has a little bacon added for flavor, but this vegan, animal-friendly recipe relies on smoked paprika to deliver the sultry and savory. If you're really missing that true bacony flavor and fatness, dial it up with house-smoked tempeh (p. 139).

Tacu tacu is meant to doll up leftovers, so use any cooked rice you have, including from last night's takeaway. Canary beans are the go-to beans in Peru, but other mild beans will do. If you've got leftover beans in the fridge, like, say, feijoada (p. 85) or Cuban black beans (p. 88) use them. They'll be delicious. Canned beans work too. Finally, the mild chile heat in your usual tacu tacu comes from Peru's aji amarillo, but a splash of your favorite hot sauce will do the job nicely.

How to serve: Tacu tacu is good any time you're hungry. It's a little more involved to make than scrambled tofu (p. 9), but it's got more substance and style. Whip it up on a busy weeknight. Any leftovers are welcome after a late night—trust me on this. It needs something green, like collard confetti (p. 57) or sukuma wiki (p. 128).

Ingredients

- 4 teaspoons olive oil, divided use
- 1 medium onion, chopped
- 1 garlic clove, chopped
- 1 cup brown rice, cooked and cooled
- 2 cups beans, cooked and cooled or 1 15-ounce can beans
- 1 teaspoon smoked paprika
- 1 teaspoon aji amarillo paste or your favorite hot sauce
- 1 sprig oregano leaves or 1/2 teaspoon dried oregano
- sea salt and fresh ground pepper

Instructions

- In a medium skillet, preferably cast iron, heat 2 teaspoons of the olive oil over medium-high heat. When the oil starts to shimmer, add the chopped onion. Sauté, stirring occasionally, until onion softens and starts to turn golden and fragrant, about 4–5 minutes. Add the garlic and stir for another minute or so, until the garlic softens. Set aside briefly to cool.
- Pour all the cooked rice and 1 cup of the cooked beans into a food processor. Add the onion mixture, the smoked paprika, hot sauce, oregano, sea salt, and freshly ground pepper. Pulse a few times—the mixture should be thick, coarse, and pebbly in texture, rather than a smooth purée.

- In a large bowl, stir together the rice and beans mixture with the remaining cup of beans. This makes for a tacu tacu with more oomph and character. Taste again for salt and pepper. Preheat oven to 400°F.
- Pour the remaining 2 teaspoons of olive oil into the skillet. Heat over medium high-heat, then spoon the rice and beans into the skillet, smoothing the top evenly. Cook over medium-high heat until it starts to set and bubbles slightly at the edges, about 10 minutes.
- Using potholders, move the skillet into the oven and continue baking for another 20 minutes, or until tacu tacu is set and slightly crusty. Remember, crust is the point of potcake. Flip the tacu tacu onto a plate if you're feeling bold, or nudge it out gently with a spatula. It should come out clean. If it sticks, no worries, just pat any stray bits back into place.
- Serves 2 to 4.

Miami Favorites—Caribbean Pigeon Peas and Rice

Traditionally, this dish is made with pigeon peas—cute, round, and tan, also called gandules, or the fun name, gungo peas. They're a staple in markets with Latin American and Caribbean communities. If you can't find them, no worries. Use red beans (another island favorite) instead. No harm will be done.

As with tacu tacu (p. 90). the beans and rice need to be cooked in advance before you start this dish. Plan ahead. In fact, the whole dish can be made ahead and reheated when you're ready to serve.

How to serve: Caribbean pigeon peas and rice is a happy-making one-pot meal on a weeknight, but it can be dressed up with a green salad dressed with tamarind vinaigrette (p. 124) or tropical slaw (p. 58) and served with cornbread (p. 34). Add a dollop of papaya chutney (p. 120) or pikliz (p. 122), and you've got a party.

Ingredients

- 2 cups pigeon peas or red beans, cooked and cooled or 1 15-ounce can of beans, rinsed and drained
- 2-1/2 cups brown rice, cooked and cooled
- 2 tablespoons olive oil
- 1 large onion, chopped (about 2 cups)
- 3 garlic cloves, chopped
- 1 green or red pepper, chopped (about 1 cup)
- 1/4 (Scotch bonnet pepper, minced or 1 to 2 jalapeños, seeded and chopped, depending on how hot you like it*
- 2 celery stalks, chopped (about 1-1/2 cups)
- 1 tomato, chopped (or 1 cup canned chopped tomatoes, drained)
- 1 teaspoon allspice
- 1/2 teaspoon cumin
- 1 small handful fresh thyme leaves or 1/4 teaspoon dried
- 1 small bunch cilantro, coarsely chopped
- sea salt and fresh ground pepper to taste

Instructions

- In a large skillet, heat the oil over medium-high heat. Add the onion and garlic, and sauté until softened, about 5 minutes. Add the chile and celery, and continue cooking, stirring occasionally, for another 5 minutes. Stir in the chopped tomato and season with the allspice and cumin.
- Add the cooked pigeon peas and rice, stirring until the mixture is well combined. Reduce the heat to medium and continue cooking, stirring occasionally, until the moisture from the vegetables is absorbed, about 10 minutes. Add the thyme, cilantro, sea salt, and pepper.
- Serves 4 to 6. Doubles beautifully.

Miami Favorites—Fideuà or Fideos

Say what? Oh, honey, I can't pronounce it either, but it's a terrific Spanish dish that's great for a party. Call it fideos—most people around here do. It's kin to paella (p. 96), but instead of rice, you make it with broken, toasted fideos or angel hair pasta. Like paella, it's often studded with seafood. Here, optional nori gives it a briny taste and lets fish be fish.

How to serve: Making fideuà is a little fiddly, but prep, including pan-toasting the angel hair and preparing the sauce it's finished in, can be done ahead. Then reintroduce the pasta and sauce and cook them together for just 15 minutes. Nice by itself or if you want something green, as I always do, serve with a green salad or Catalan spinach (p. 55)

Ingredients

- 3 cups vegetable broth or water
- 1 sheet nori for a mildly fishy but vegan flavor (optional)
- 3 tablespoons olive oil
- 1 small onion, diced (about 3/4 cup)
- 1 red pepper, diced (about 1 cup)
- 3 garlic cloves, minced
- 1/2 teaspoon fennel seeds
- 1 teaspoon sweet paprika
- 1 good pinch saffron
- 3 tablespoons tomato paste
- 8 ounces angel hair pasta or fideos, broken into 2-inch pieces
- 1/2 cup red wine*
- 1 cup peas (frozen and thawed are fine) or chickpeas (optional)
- sea salt and fresh ground pepper

Instructions

- If you'd like to give your fideos a little taste of the sea, infuse your fideos with the nori. Pour the broth into a large pot and bring to a simmer over medium heat. Drop in the nori, cover pot with a lid, and turn off the heat. Let the broth sit for 10 minutes so the nori infuses. Some of the nori may dissolve into the broth. This is fine. Fish out and discard any extra. Then set aside.

---

* If you'd prefer not to use wine, substitute an extra half-cup of water or vegetable broth.

- Now, on to the fideos. In a large skillet with straight sides, heat 1 tablespoon of olive oil over medium-high heat. Snap the dried angel hair or fideos or thin spaghetti into 2-inch pieces and add to the skillet, giving it all a careful stir so all the pasta gets a little oil.
- Toast the pasta, stirring occasionally until it darkens to deep brown and smells toasty, 8 to 10 minutes. Pour toasted pasta into a large bowl and set aside.
- Return the emptied skillet to the burner. Add the remaining 2 tablespoons of olive oil and the diced onion. Give the onion a stir with a large mixing spoon so it gets a gilding of olive oil and cook until onion softens and turns golden. Reduce heat to medium, and add the fennel seeds, minced garlic, and diced red pepper. Cook, stirring occasionally, until the vegetables soften, about 10 minutes.
- Add the toasted angel hair back to the pot. Pour in the broth and wine (or an additional 1/2 cup vegetable broth or water), work in the tomato paste, and sprinkle in the paprika. Turn heat to medium-high and combine everything gently so the pasta starts to rehydrate and soften. When everything comes to a simmer, sprinkle in the saffron, which blooms in warm liquid.
- Cook, stirring occasionally for another 8–10 minutes, until the pasta drinks up most of the liquid, and what's left is rich sauce thickened from the starchy pasta—just enough to coat the pasta.
- Now add optional peas or chickpeas, season lavishly with sea salt and fresh pepper, give it all a good toss, and serve.
- Serves 4 to 6.

Miami Favorites—Paella

Paella is a party dish, and Miami loves to party. We even have catering companies that'll show up at your event and make paella in a paella pan sometimes big enough to swim in. The result tends to be a lot of oily rice. Its richness and yellow tinge doesn't come from saffron, but from Sazon, a commercial blend of salt, cumin, and annatto—along with pork, chicken, seafood, and all manner of animal bits. It makes for a fun performance and feeds a crowd, but it's not vegan, nor is it true paella.

True paella is all about the rice, or as a Madrid chef told me, the rice is the hero of the paella. The hero's name is Bomba. Bomba is white, short-grained, thirsty, and pricy. I'm cheap, but when I make paella, I go for Bomba. It can cost up to—brace yourself—4 times more than plain white rice, but it's specially grown in Valencia, the home of paella, and absorbs 4-5 times more liquid than regular rice. It's what you need for a truly heroic paella. It's sold at specialty markets and online on its own or often as part of a paella kit, with saffron and a thin-bottomed, two-handled paella pan.

That said, I've had success making paella in a large, shallow skillet that better fits the burner on my stovetop. In either case, the rice cooks in a thin layer, not a deep pile, so it's caramelized, not steamed, and every grain is infused with the saffron-scented sofrito. If in the cooking, the rice gets crusty on the bottom, that's a win. It's called soccorat, the same thing as potcake (p. 90), and Miami is all about potcake, remember?

How to serve: I sometimes stud my finished paella with artichoke hearts, chickpeas, and strips of roasted red peppers because I can't resist adding more vegetables. If you want your paella pure and heroic, serve with parrillada de verduras (roasted assorted vegetables) with chimichurri (p. 123), and a bold, musky Rioja. The Rioja can have some age on it, but the paella shouldn't. Serve as soon as it's ready.

Ingredients

- 5 cups vegetable broth
- 1 sheet nori or strip kombu
- 1 dried ñora or ancho chile*
- 1/4 cup olive oil
- 1 small onion, chopped small (about 3/4 cup)
- 1 red pepper, chopped small (about 1 cup)
- 2 garlic cloves, minced
- 1/2 teaspoon sweet paprika
- 2 pinches saffron
- 1/2 cup diced tomato (canned is fine)
- sea salt and fresh ground pepper
- 1 cup Bomba rice

---

* Ñora, a mild Spanish chile, is available in some specialty markets. Ancho is a fine alternative, and more widely available.

Instructions

- Pour the broth into a large pot. Add the nori or kombu and bring to a simmer over medium-high heat. Reduce heat to low, cover, and allow the seaweed to infuse the broth for at least 10 minutes and up to 30 minutes. Remove the seaweed and set the broth aside.
- Drop ñora or ancho into a small bowl. Cover with boiling water to rehydrate. Set aside.
- Pour the olive oil into a 10-inch paella pan or skillet. Heat pan over medium heat. Add chopped onion, red pepper, and garlic. Give the vegetables a stir with a large mixing spoon, preferably wooden, so everything gets a gilding of olive oil. Then reduce heat to low and cook gently, until vegetables soften and give off some liquid, about 10 minutes.
- Fish out the dried chile and remove the stem and seeds. Chop well and drop it into the pan. Add the paprika, chopped tomato, and saffron. Sauté, stirring, until all the vegetable liquid evaporates and the oil comes to the surface again—about 10 minutes.
- Pour in the rice, and mix so each grain of rice glistens with sofrito. Season generously with sea salt and pepper. Gently pour in the vegetable broth. It will totally drown the rice at first. Take heart.
- Spread rice evenly over the bottom of the pan. Now stop stirring and let it be. Bring to a boil over medium-high heat and cook, uncovered, for 10 minutes, then lower the heat to medium and let the paella simmer for a minimum of 10 minutes, to let the Bomba rice absorb all the broth and flavors.
- Your paella will tell you it's almost ready when the rice has absorbed most of the broth and the top of the paella appears dry. Now it's time for your paella to rest. Turn off the heat but leave the pan on the burner. Cover with a clean dish cloth, or even a thick section of newspaper for 10 minutes, then serve at once.
- Serves 4.

Miami Flavors—Angel Hair with Pumpkin, Annatto, and Lime

My friend raves about her abuela's chicken noodle soup, a savory broth golden with annatto, turmeric, and cumin, strands of fideos—skinny noodles like angel hair pasta—accessorized with calabaza and other vegetables and finished with lime. The problem is the chicken. I've kept the mellowness, the comfort, and the tropical spice and citrus zings, but lost the chicken. And the soup. The result is a pleasing pasta dish that saves you time and saves a chicken, too.

How to serve: Have a bowl of lime quarters and a bottle of good extra virgin olive oil on the table for extra zip.

Ingredients

- 2 tablespoons olive oil
- 1 onion, diced (about 1-1/2 cups)
- 2 garlic cloves, minced
- 1 pound calabaza or other winter pumpkin, peeled and diced (about 2 cups)
- 1 red pepper, diced (about 1 cup)
- 1 celery stalk, diced (about 1/2 cup)
- 1/2 teaspoon turmeric
- 1 teaspoon annatto or pinch saffron
- 1 teaspoon cumin
- 1 teaspoon coriander
- 1 tomato, diced or 1/2 pint grape tomatoes, halved
- 1 cup vegetable broth
- 8 ounces fideos,* angel hair pasta, or thin spaghetti, preferably whole wheat
- 1 cup reserved pasta water
- 1/2 cup cilantro chopped
- 2 tablespoons fresh lime juice
- sea salt and fresh ground pepper

---

* Fideos are available in many grocery stores in the pasta section, at specialty markets, and online. Angel hair pasta makes a fine substitute.

Instructions

- In a large skillet, heat olive oil over medium-high heat. Add diced onion and cook, stirring, just until it starts to soften, about 4 minutes.
- Add minced garlic and diced pumpkin, and sauté. Add the pepper and celery and stir so the vegetables glisten.
- Add the tomato and broth. When everything comes to a gentle boil, sprinkle in the spices and stir to combine.
- Reduce heat and simmer, stirring occasionally, until the vegetables are softened, and the broth is slightly reduced, about 10 minutes. Set aside. May be done an hour or two ahead, and kept covered until you're ready to make the pasta.
- For the pasta, bring a large pot of water to boil. When it reaches a vigorous boil, add fideos or angel hair, and cook for 4–5 minutes, or just until al dente. Skinny pasta is quick-cooking pasta.
- Drain pasta, reserving one cup of pasta cooking water. Return the drained pasta to the empty pot, then add the vegetables and broth. Give it all a good toss.
- Add the lime juice and chopped cilantro. Season lavishly with sea salt and pepper.
- If pasta needs a little more sauciness, add 1/4 cup of the pasta water, toss again, and serve at once.
- Serves 3 to 4. Doubles easily.

Miami Favorites—Sort of Sancocho

It's Puerto Rican. It's Colombian. It's Dominican. It's a freewheeling everything-in-the-pot soup. Or stew. It's a sign of celebration. It's sancocho, and it's likely to be *Miami Vegan*'s most contentious recipe. Miami folks love sancocho, everybody makes it differently, everyone swears theirs (or their mami's or their abuela's) is the best. No two recipes are the same.

Technique and ingredients may vary, and are wildly proprietary, anyway, but sancocho usually contains corn, plantains, calabaza, and tropical tubers like yuca, yam, and malanga. Also possibly chicken, goat, pork or beef. Not here it doesn't. So, then, can you lose the meat but keep the mmmmm? And more importantly, keep the soul? Some people advise adding seitan, miso, vegan sausage, or nutritional yeast to replace the meat and provide umami punch. Their versions may be excellent, but to me, they veer too far off Miami's sancocho trail. I let the vegetables do the talking.

You may ask what makes this sancocho instead of, say, a really good vegetable soup or stew. The tropical tubers, the annatto, and, I hope, the spirit. Everyone has their own sancocho recipe. This is mine.

How to serve: Traditionally, the corn goes into the sancocho on the cob, cut into 2-inch pieces. This makes for an Instagram-worthy presentation, but a challenge to eat. I have further broken with tradition by putting the whole corn in for flavor, then cutting the corn off the cob to serve.

Spoon rice, preferably the brown kind, into soup bowls and ladle sancocho on top.

Finish with sliced avocado, a squeeze of lime juice and hot sauce

To make it more of a party, serve with little bowls of diced avocado, chopped onion, lime quarters, and a bottle of hot sauce, and let everyone dress up their own customized bowl.

Ingredients

- 2 tablespoons olive oil
- 1 large onion, chopped (about 1-1/2 cups)
- 4 garlic cloves, chopped
- 1 red, orange, or yellow pepper, chopped (about 1 cup)
- 1 pound calabaza, peeled and chopped
- 1/2 pound yam or sweet potato, chopped
- 1 green plantain, sliced
- 2 ears corn
- 6 cups vegetable broth
- 4 tablespoons tomato paste
- 1 tablespoon annatto
- sea salt and fresh ground pepper
- 1 bunch cilantro, chopped

Instructions

- Heat olive oil in a large soup pot over medium-high heat. Add the chopped onion, garlic pepper, and cook stirring for a few minutes, until vegetables soften and become fragrant, about 8–10 minutes.
- Add the chopped calabaza, yam, and plantain, and stir just to soften, about 5 minutes. Pour in the broth, spoon in the tomato paste and annatto. Stir to combine, then add the two whole ears of corn.
- Bring everything to a boil, then reduce heat to low and simmer uncovered for 45 minutes to an hour. Sancocho will have thickened.
- Season generously with sea salt, ground pepper, and chopped cilantro.
- When ready to serve, slice the corn off the cobs, then press the knife blade against the cobs to release the rich corn broth back into the sancocho. .Discard or compost the cobs and ladle up your sancocho.
- Serves 6.

Collards

Southerners love their greens. But sometimes, we hurt the ones we love. The traditional way to cook collards in the South is to throw them into a pot of boiling salt water with a hunk of pig. Then the greens simmer until the leaves limp, gray, and defeated. A splash of vinegar and/or Crystal hot sauce does little to revive them.

Collard greens can handle abuse, though. Consider their torturous growing conditions—high heat, direct sun, occasional drought, and risk of assorted insect infestations. Collards don't care. They thrive. Mine don't even seem to mind when our dog leaps over them or plows right through them. Still, once they make it to the kitchen, I say collards earn kinder treatment.

Rather than being boiled till they give up, collards' very greenness shines when they meet gentle heat. Pair with sweet roots and winter squashes, or creamy grits (p. 132). They need no animal. They're even delicious raw (p. 61). Yes, really.

Miami Flavors—Collard Tacos with Chile-Charred Onion and Sweet Potato

Collards greens' bold flavors make them a tough solo act, but mellow them with roasted sweet potatoes and onions tickled with chile and you've got a tortilla-worthy trio.

How to serve: Kale works as well as collards; pumpkin or other winter squash can sub for sweet potato. Serve with tortillas—corn and collards love each other, but good flour ones work too. Tacos are most fun when everyone can design their own. Serve with little bowls of fixings such as:

- chopped avocado
- thinly sliced radish
- chopped tomato
- chopped cilantro
- toasted pumpkin seeds
- shredded vegan cheese
- refried beans
- salsa

Ingredients

- 8 ounces collard leaves, tough stems removed and reserved for another use*
- 2 teaspoons olive oil
- 1 tablespoon garlic, minced
- 2 teaspoons cumin seeds
- a sliver of Scotch bonnet or serrano or 1 jalapeno, minced if desired
- 3/4 cup water or vegetable broth
- sea salt and fresh ground pepper
- 1–2 sweet potatoes, diced (about 2 cups)
- 2 large onions, sliced in half then again into half-moons (about 2 cups)
- 2 teaspoons chile powder
- 2 tablespoons olive oil
- sea salt
- the juice of one lime juicy to finish
- 6–8 tortillas

---

*Use to make vegetable broth or add to compost.

Instructions

- Use a Vitamix, the shred blade of a food processor, or your impressive knife skills to shred collards into little confetti-like bits. Shredding helps keep them of a manageable size to eat and helps break down their cell walls so they become more tender. You'll notice the greens darken and shrink down. You should have about 5 cups.
- In a large skillet, preferably cast iron, heat the 2 teaspoons of olive oil over medium-high heat. Add the minced garlic and cumin seeds. Cook, stirring for a few minutes, until the garlic softens and turns golden and the cumin seeds release their fragrance.
- Add the shredded collards and stir well, letting the greens settle into the skillet. Add the optional minced chile.
- Pour in the 3/4 cup water and stir. Reduce heat to medium and let the greens cook down until softened and all the liquid is absorbed, about 15–20 minutes. Give them the occasional stir to avoid sticking or burning. Set aside.
- Preheat oven to 425°F. Line 2 rimmed baking sheets with parchment paper or Silpats.
- In a large bowl, mix together the diced sweet potato and sliced onions. Drizzle in the 2 tablespoons olive oil and sprinkle in the chile powder. Season with sea salt and fresh ground pepper and stir or toss to combine.
- Spread out the vegetables into the 2 baking sheets, taking care not to crowd. Roast for about 20–25 minutes, stirring once halfway through. Onions and sweet potatoes should be burnished, softened, and slightly charred at the tips.
- Spread each tortilla with a heaping spoonful of collard greens. Top with a large spoonful of the onions and sweet potato. Let everyone garnish with desired accompaniments.
- Serves 6.

Miami Flavors—Collard Parcels with Chile Pecan Rice

Collard greens show off their elegant side. Their broad leaves become the natural packages for creamy chile pecan rice.

How to serve: Collard parcels can be made several hours ahead and refrigerated, then baked off just before serving. This makes them a perfect dinner party dish—that and the fact they look stylish on the plate and offer wow in every bite—creamy, nutty, and herbaceous, with a whisper of chile warmth. Feel free to swap rice for another cooked nubbly whole grain like farro or barley.

The collard parcels plump as they bake, so each one becomes a substantial serving. Serve with a simple green salad with tamarind vinaigrette (p. 124) and ripe sweet plantains (p. 143).

Ingredients

- 1 pound collard greens
- 2 tablespoons olive oil
- 1 good-sized onion, chopped (about 1-1/2 cups)
- 4 garlic cloves, minced
- 1 jalapeño, minced
- 4 cups brown, red, or black rice, cooked and cooled
- 2 tablespoons nutritional yeast
- 1 cup plain, unsweetened oat milk
- 3/4 cups pecans, toasted and chopped
- sea salt and fresh ground pepper to taste

Cilantro Sauce

- 1 bunch cilantro, leaves and stems (about 2 cups)
- 4 garlic cloves
- 1/4 cup olive oil
- 2 teaspoons coriander
- 1/3 cup fresh lime juice
- 1 cup water
- sea salt and fresh ground pepper

Instructions

- Preheat oven to 350°F. Have ready an oven-proof casserole or baking dish.
- Bring a large pot of salted water to boil. Slice out the thick center stems from the collards. Discard, or better, reserve them and use them to make vegetable broth.

- Blanche the collard leaves in the boiling water for about 2 minutes, then let them drain and cool in a colander.
- Meanwhile, heat olive oil in a large skillet over medium-high heat. Add the chopped onion, and stir, letting the onion cook and soften, about 5 minutes. Stir in the minced garlic and jalapeño, and continue cooking for another few minutes, until the vegetables are softened and fragrant.
- Tip in the rice and stir to combine. Add the nutritional yeast, oat milk, and pecans. Season generously with sea salt and ground pepper, and remove from heat.
- Now make the cilantro sauce. Whizz all the ingredients together in a food processor or blender for a minute or so, until they form a bright green sauce.
- On a work surface, arrange 2 collard leaves so they overlap and form an oval, more or less. Place 1/2 cup of the chili pecan rice in the center. Fold the edges of the collards over the rice like it's an envelope. Place seam-side down in the baking dish.
- Repeat with remaining collard leaves. Pour the cilantro sauce around the parcels. Cover with casserole lid or cover tightly with foil, and bake for 30 minutes.
- Serves 6 to 8. Recipe doubles easily.

Curry

I love curry the whole world over—from India, Thailand, Africa, Indonesia, Japan, Sri Lanka, and naturally, curries closer to home, like this one. Rich with coconut milk and mellow with tropical fruits and vegetables, curries from Trinidad and Jamaica will convince you not all curries are screamingly hot. These curries are more about golden warming spices like turmeric. They're sunny and friendly.

For years, I thought of curry as a dish infused with masala, a blend of warming spices like cumin, coriander, turmeric, and chile. Using commercial curry powder would be cheating. And curry certainly didn't grow on trees. Actually, it does. A member of the citrus family, curry leaf isn't spicy, but has a haunting low note, and adds an elusive but elemental dimension to every Indian dal, Thai red curry, or other curry you love. If you're in my 'hood, help yourself to fresh curry leaves from my curry leaf tree. The weedy thing I planted years ago has grown into quite a robust specimen, ever glad to offer up a few sprigs for dinner.

You can sometimes find frozen curry leaves in Indian markets, or other specialty markets. But don't struggle.

Miami Flavors—Caribbean Curry

Forgive the long list of ingredients. You can switch out the vegetables and starchy tubers for anything sturdy, like cauliflower, cabbage, and potatoes. A plus for those like me who aren't into precision chopping—chunkier chunks of vegetables and fruits work better here. Larger pieces mean they won't go to mush in the cooking, and the true taste of pineapple, plantain, and calabaza still shines through, even as they're robed in sauce. The chopped nuts and cilantro at the end really make this dish, so try not to skip them.

Jamaican curry powder, available in some grocery stores and online, is a mild turmeric-forward blend and can replace all the dried spices and seeds in this recipe. Making this with Jamaican curry powder and without curry leaves may not hit all the high and low notes but it'll still be singing the same happy song.

How to serve: Serve with brown rice, roti, or both. Keep lime quarters, lemon pickle, hot sauce, and papaya chutney (p. 120) on the table.

Ingredients

- 2 tablespoons coconut oil or neutral oil such as grapeseed
- 1 thumb-sized piece of ginger, minced
- 4 garlic cloves, minced
- 1 teaspoon Scotch bonnet pepper, minced or 1/2 jalapeño, minced
- 2 teaspoons mustard seeds
- 1-1/2 teaspoon cumin
- 1-1/2 teaspoon coriander
- 1 teaspoon turmeric
- 1 large onion, sliced (about 1-1/2 cups)
- 2 cups cauliflower or cabbage, chopped
- 2–3 carrots, chopped (about 1 cup)
- 2 cups calabaza or green plantain, chopped
- 2 tablespoons tomato paste
- 1 cup water or vegetable broth
- 1 14-ounce can full-fat coconut milk
- 1 handful fresh curry leaves (optional)
- 1 cup pineapple, chopped or half a 14-ounce can chopped pineapple
- 2 teaspoons garam masala*

---

* A gentle Indian spice blend of cumin, cardamom, cinnamon, cloves, and more. Available online and in many specialty markets.

- 1 teaspoon sea salt plus more to taste
- 2 tablespoons lime juice
- 1 bunch cilantro, chopped
- 1 handful peanuts or cashews, toasted and chopped

Instructions

- In a large soup pot, heat oil over medium-high heat. When it starts to shimmer, add the minced ginger, minced garlic, minced chili, and mustard seeds. Stir for a minute, then cover with the lid. After a few minutes, the mustard seeds will start to pop and ping from the heat, releasing flavor. When they've quieted down, reduce heat to low, lift the lid, and add the cumin, coriander, and turmeric or a goodly tablespoon of Jamaican curry powder. Stir together, then add the sliced onion and chopped cauliflower, carrots and calabaza.
- Cook, stirring now and again, until the vegetables soften, turning fragrant, and take on a soft, golden hue from the turmeric-spiced oil, about 5–8 minutes.
- Now add the tomato paste and water or broth, stirring to combine. When the tomato paste has dissolved, pour in the coconut milk, stir, and allow everything to come to a low boil. Drop in the sprig of curry leaves, if you have it. Reduce heat to low, allow the curry flavors to blend (you know, making a masala), and infuse the vegetables, for 25 minutes. The vegetables should be tender, but not mushy.
- Add the chopped pineapple and garam masala, the sea salt and the lime juice. Stir again to combine and taste for balance.
- Before serving, top with chopped cilantro and/or a handful of chopped toasted peanuts or cashews.
- Serves 6.

Miami Favorites—Vegan Macaroni and Cheese

Miami is full of transplants from elsewhere. We all bring our own foodways with us, and in time, they all mix together. That's what makes Miami so delicious and dynamic. Same thing goes for macaroni and cheese. A French dish introduced to America thanks to James Hemings, Thomas Jefferson's enslaved Black chef, we now think of mac and cheese as a comforting all-American dish beloved by all. Thanks to quality commercial plant-based milk and cheese that includes vegans too.

How to serve: Crusty, gooey, easy, cheesy, and vegan, this is a one-pot wonder. Add a green salad, sukuma wiki (p. 128) or tropical slaw (p. 58) and you're ready for action.

Ingredients

- 1/2 cup toasted breadcrumbs
- 8 ounces (1/2 pound) short pasta—elbow macaroni, penne, fusilli, whatever you like—preferably whole wheat
- 4 tablespoons vegan butter (1/2 stick)
- 1/4 cup unbleached all-purpose flour
- 2 cups unsweetened oat milk
- 1/4 cup nutritional yeast
- sea salt and fresh ground pepper
- 1 cup shredded vegan cheddar

Instructions

- Preheat oven to 350°F. Lightly oil a deep ovenproof casserole or baking dish. Sprinkle most of the breadcrumbs at the bottom of the casserole, reserving about 3 tablespoons for later.
- Bring a large pot of water to a rolling boil. Pour in the pasta and cook a few minutes less than package directions, so it's still firm, but not crunchy. It will continue to cook in the oven. Drain pasta well and set aside.
- In a medium saucepan, melt vegan butter over medium-high heat. Pour in the unbleached flour and stir until you have a smooth paste.
- Pour in the oat milk and nutritional yeast, and continue to stir until you have a thick, velvety sauce. Season generously with sea salt and ground pepper. Tumble the pasta into the baking dish. Pour the sauce over everything. Season again with sea salt and pepper, and scatter shredded cheddar over all. Top with remaining breadcrumbs.
- Bake mac and cheese for 20 minutes or until everything's heated through and bubbly and crumb topping is golden brown.
- Serves 4. Doubles easily.

Extras, Sides, and Salsas

Miami Flavors—Mango Barbecue Sauce

Barbecue sauce is where even chill folk take a hard stand, where they're do-or-die loyal to their own, whether it's white Alabama barbecue sauce or Carolina vinegar-based. Florida's own Zora Neale Hurston, novelist, anthropologist, and legend wrote the origin of barbecue sauce came from Africa by way of the Caribbean—a tart, potent mix of citrus and chile. I added mango to the mix when I had some mango purée left after making a loaf of mango bread (p. 19). Mango of course adds an element of sweetness, but the apple cider vinegar and tamari add balance.

How to serve: Brush on grilled or roasted green plantains, cauliflower, or house-smoked tempeh (p. 139)

Ingredients

- 1 tablespoon olive oil
- 1 small onion, chopped fine (about 1/2 cup)
- 2 cloves garlic, minced
- 1 teaspoon jalapeño (2 teaspoons if you're feeling bold), minced
- 1/2 cup mango purée
- 1-1/2 cup tomato purée
- 1/4 cup apple cider vinegar
- 2 tablespoons molasses
- 1 teaspoon tamari, soy sauce, or liquid aminos
- 1/2 teaspoon chili powder
- 1 teaspoon smoked paprika
- 1/4 teaspoon sea salt or to taste

Instructions

- Heat olive oil in a large pot over medium heat. Add chopped onion and cook slowly, stirring until the onion mellows, softens, and turns translucent, 5–8 minutes. Add minced garlic and jalapeño. Cook, stirring for another 3 minutes, just until the garlic and jalapeño soften. The lower heat keeps the vegetables from burning, which adds a harsh note.
- Stir in the mango and tomato purées. Turn the heat up to medium-high and cook just until mixture comes to a boil. Add apple cider vinegar, molasses, tamari, chili powder, smoked paprika, and sea salt. Stir and reduce heat to low. Simmer, uncovered for 1 hour. The sauce will thicken and go from bright red to a rich brick tone.
- Allow the barbecue sauce to cool slightly. Taste again and add more sea salt if desired.
- Makes about 2 cups.

# Papaya

Papaya is a tropical fruit that leads two lives. On the outside, it's an awkward combination of long and bulbous, with green and yellow striated skin. Its charms become apparent when you slice it in half lengthwise. Then you discover its creamy flesh in blushing sunset colors, and a central cavity brimming with glossy seeds like black pearls. It's like finding treasure.

When young, firm, and green, papaya, like mango and plantain, tastes more like a vegetable. When it's softer and riper, papaya becomes mildly sweet—maybe more mild than sweet—and perfumy (with a slightly funky underscent).

Papaya skin needs to be peeled prior to eating, and unlike melon rind, it peels away easily. Even better, in the wonderful symbiotic way of nature, rubbing the inside of papaya peel on your face is a free spa treatment, its enzymes zipping away dead skin and other nasties. Eating the fruit is beautifying, too. It's rich in A, B, C, and E, your best vitamins for radiance and sexuality, as well as enzymes, minerals, and phytoestrogens.

Miami Flavors—20-Minute Golden Papaya Chutney

My first taste of chutney came from a family friend when I was little. In memory, at least, it glowed golden in the spoon as I toddled up to her to taste. Nothing prepared me for that explosion of wow, of sweet tropical fruit, slight tang, warm spices, and crunchy nuts. As I grew older, I'd help her make her special holiday batch for family and friends, a sweltering day-long enterprise involving peeling, slicing, chopping, measuring, and stirring the pot as it simmers. It simmers for a long time.

Then comes sterilizing jars for canning, and carefully pouring the chutney into them for minimal waste and mess, but even so, the kitchen's a disaster zone anyway. Then comes the industrial-grade clean-up. I'm saying I appreciate what goes into a good chutney.

The papaya in this recipe glows golden with turmeric, but technically, it's not a true chutney, since it doesn't contain vinegar as a preserving agent and doesn't involve a long, hot day of cooking and canning. This to me is a plus. It is, however, true to chutney in that it's tangy, fruity, a little spicy, and a little nutty (like me).

How to serve: Enjoy this chunky sauce dolloped on avocado toast or slathered on pumpkin bread (p. 28), hoecakes (p. 32), or cornbread (p. 34).

Ingredients

- 1 tablespoon coconut oil or grapeseed or other neutral oil
- 1 teaspoon brown mustard seeds
- 1-1/2 teaspoons allspice
- 1-1/2 teaspoons turmeric
- 1 onion, halved then sliced into skinny half-moons (about 1 cup)
- 2 garlic cloves, minced
- 1 thumb-sized piece of ginger, minced
- 1/2 jalapeño, minced
- 1 nice, ripe papaya, peeled, seeded, and chopped (about 2 cups)
- juice of 1 to 2 limes (about 2 tablespoons)
- sea salt to taste
- 1 handful of cilantro, chopped
- 1 good sprig of mint leaves, (about 2 teaspoons), chopped
- 1/3 cup roasted cashews, chopped

Instructions

- Heat oil in a large skillet over medium-high heat until it starts to shimmer. Add the mustard seeds, allspice, and turmeric. Stir, then cover with a lid. After a few minutes, you'll hear the mustard seeds pop from the heat, releasing flavor. When they've quieted down, lift the lid and add the thinly sliced onion, and minced garlic, ginger, and jalapeño.
- Cook, stirring now and again, until the vegetables soften, turning fragrant and taking on a soft golden hue from the turmeric-spiced oil, about 5–8 minutes.
- Add chopped papaya and lime juice, stirring just to heat through, and let the papaya soften.
- Season generously with sea salt. Stir in chopped cilantro and mint and sprinkle in chopped cashews.
- Serves 4 to 6.

Miami Flavors—Nori Dust

Recipes like Bahamian chowder (p. 69) and smoked sea dip (p. 29) call for a certain marine taste. Using seaweed achieves fishy flavor without the fish.

Ingredients

- 1/2 sheet nori*
- Preheat oven to 300°F.

Instructions

- Place the nori sheet on a baking sheet. Pop it in the oven for 10 minutes or until it shrinks and smells toasty and of the sea. Give it a minute to cool slightly, crush it up with a mortar and pestle or small spice grinder till you have something looking like black confetti, and you're done.
- Makes about 1/2 cup. Store in an airtight container. It keeps indefinitely.

---

* Available in some specialty markets and grocery stores.

Miami Favorites—Pikliz

It's a sauce, it's a relish, it's a veg-intense condiment you'll find in almost every Haitian home in every South Florida Haitian restaurant. Pikliz (pronounced pik-LEEZ) makes the most out of heat-resistant summer crops like carrots, cabbage, chiles, and onions. It looks like cole slaw, but don't fall for that. It packs a Scotch bonnet sucker punch. Adding a second Scotch bonnet makes it truer to the Haitian ideal. Unless you can truly stand the heat, start with one.

It seems easier to bung all the vegetables in the food processor, but if possible, resist the temptation. Hand chopping the vegetables results in crisper, more authentic pikliz. This quick fuss-free pickle will be ready to eat after 48 hours, but flavors will bloom the longer you keep it. And you can keep it indefinitely. Enjoy a spoonful or two of pikliz on just about anything, including sos pwa (p. 68), djon djon rice (p. 73), and collard tacos (p. 105).

Ingredients

- 2 cups cabbage, about half a pound, thinly sliced
- 1 carrot, diced (about 1/2 cup)
- 1 red pepper, diced (about 1/2 cup)
- 1 onion, diced (about 3/4 cup)
- 1–2 Scotch bonnet peppers, minced
- 1 teaspoon sea salt
- 2/3 cup orange juice
- 1/3 cup lime juice
- 1 cup cider vinegar
- 4 whole cloves
- 4 whole garlic cloves
- 1/4 teaspoon whole black peppercorns

Instructions

- In a large bowl, mix together the sliced cabbage, diced carrot, pepper, and onion, and minced Scotch bonnet. Sprinkle in sea salt and toss to combine. Pour in the orange juice, lime juice, and cider vinegar. Vegetables should be just about submerged. Give them a stir and drop in the cloves, garlic cloves, and peppercorns.
- Pour everything into a 1-quart Mason jar or similar glass container with a tight-fitting lid. Refrigerate for a couple of days, giving the jar an occasional shake when you think to.
- Makes 4 cups.

Miami Favorites—Chimichurri

Chimichurri is the national sauce of Argentina, a bright green condiment that, like Haitian pikliz (p. 122) punches above its weight. Everyone has their own magic blend, but at core, it's parsley and/or cilantro, garlic, lemon, vinegar, and olive oil. Some chimichurris are sharper, others are oilier. Maybe you add minced chile (I do), maybe you add minced onion.

Freshly made chimichurri is a cooling emerald green, with a little herbal edge, but it is not yet delicious. The mellow green herbs are a little intimidated by their bolder fellow ingredients, and the result is unbalanced. Just wait.

Cover and refrigerate for an hour or up to overnight, so the ingredients can get to know each other. Chimichurri darkens and thickens during refrigeration, but the flavor balance will be just right.

How to serve: This is the sauce you need to wake up any vegetable. Especially good to drizzle on roasted potatoes (p. 126) or chickpea tofu (p. 49). I sometimes use it as a salad dressing too.

Ingredients

- 1 cup cilantro, coarsely chopped
- 1/2 cup flatleaf parsley, coarsely chopped
- 4 cloves garlic
- 1/2 jalapeño or 1 teaspoon serrano, minced
- 2 tablespoons red wine vinegar
- 2 tablespoons lemon juice
- 3/4 cup olive oil
- 1 teaspoon salt

Instructions

- Pulse the cilantro, parsley, garlic, and chile in a food processor just a few times, so all the bits are like confetti, small but not smooshed.
- Pour in the red wine, vinegar, and lemon juice. Pulse again.
- Now with the processing blade running, add the salt and slowly pour in the olive oil.
- Whiz until everything's combined. Chimichurri should be bright green, thick but pourable, and have an appealingly herbaceous scent.
- Pour into a jar with a tight-fitting lid. Cover and refrigerate for 1 hour or pretty much as long as you like.
- Makes 1 cup.

Miami Flavors—Tamarind Vinaigrette

A little tamarind hit mellowed with orange brings some dazzle to dressing. Can't find tamarind? Fabulous faux—molasses with a squeeze of lime.

How to serve: Zing up a simple green salad. A current favorite around these parts is spinach salad with avocado, orange, and hearts of palm.

Ingredients

- 1 tablespoon tamarind concentrate
- 1/3 cup orange juice
- 1 teaspoon apricot or peach jam
- 3 tablespoons olive oil

Instructions

- In a small bowl, stir together tamarind, orange juice, and jam until tamarind and jam dissolve and incorporate into the juice. Then stir in the olive oil. Add a pinch of sea salt if you like. For best results, pour into a jar with a tight-fitting lid and let it refrigerate for an hour or so to let flavors blend.
- Makes 1/2 cup, more than enough for a large salad.

Miami Flavors—Summer Squash Casserole

Miami is modern, multicultural, Michelin-starred, glitzy, and *Real Housewives*-y, but in the dead of summer when the tourists flee, you can still glimpse the sleepy Southern town it used to be a century ago—no A/C, no Airbnb. Miami Beach had hotels, but the mainland mostly had—get this—boarding houses. One of them, Hopkins House, was famous for its squash casserole. Summer squash, also known as yellow squash, is not the most exciting vegetable, and the original recipe called for boiling it. There was no cream sauce, no flurry of herbs. But people lined up for it. This plant-based version keeps that retro vibe but opts for cooking the summer squash in a skillet rather than boiling the dickens out of it.

How to serve: This casserole belongs as part of a great Southern mixed plate, with sides like tropical slaw (p. 58), cowboy caviar (p. 136), and a wedge of cornbread (p. 34).

Ingredients

- 2 tablespoons vegan butter
- 1 large onion, chopped (about 1 cup)
- 3 cloves garlic, minced
- 1-2 good-sized summer squash, chopped (about 2-1/2 cups)
- pinch red pepper flakes
- 1 tablespoon nutritional yeast
- 1/2 cup cracker crumbs
- sea salt and fresh ground pepper to taste

Instructions

- Preheat oven to 350°F. Lightly oil a 6-cup ovenproof casserole or baking dish.
- Pour chopped summer squash into a colander or sieve. Sprinkle with coarse salt and place over a bowl or in the sink. Let it sit for at least 15 minutes. This draws out the squash's excess water, avoids mushiness, and makes for denser, more satisfying squash. Rinse well and blot dry.
- Melt vegan butter in a large skillet over medium-high heat. When it starts to sizzle, add the chopped onion. Sauté, stirring occasionally, until golden. Add the minced garlic and the summer squash
- Continue cooking, stirring occasionally, until the squash softens, and breaks down about 5–8 minutes. Add the red pepper flakes, nutritional yeast, and about half the cracker crumbs, reserving the rest for the top.
- Stir to combine and season generously with sea salt and pepper.
- Spoon the squash into the prepared casserole dish. Sprinkle the remaining cracker crumbs on top.
- Bake for 20 minutes or until the cracker crumbs are golden brown and the casserole is heated through.
- Serves 4.

Miami Favorites—Roasted Potatoes—Papas Asada

Some roasted potato recipes tell you to just bung the potatoes in the oven, but I find parboiling them for just a few minutes before roasting means your potatoes don't dry out. You get crispy potato outside and tender potato inside.

How to serve: Papas asada are a basic go-to side dish. But they're mighty fine with chimichurri (p. 123) drizzled on top. Get 'em while they're hot.

Ingredients

- 1-1/2 pounds small new potatoes, or 2 russet potatoes
- 2 teaspoons paprika
- 2 teaspoons garlic powder
- 1 teaspoon fresh thyme leaves or 1/2 teaspoon dried thyme
- 2 tablespoons olive oil
- 1/2 teaspoon sea salt, plus more to finish
- fresh ground pepper to taste

Instructions

- Preheat oven to 425°F. Prepare a rimmed baking sheet with parchment or a Silpat.
- If using russet potatoes, slice into bite-sized pieces. Small potatoes can be left whole.
- Cover potatoes with cold water in a large pot. Bring to boil over medium-high heat and let the potatoes cook for 8–10 minutes until they just start to soften.
- Drain potatoes well.
- In a large bowl, whisk together the paprika, garlic powder, thyme, olive oil, and sea salt. Add the potatoes while still warm. Gently mix and let the potatoes sit for 15 minutes to absorb the spices.
- Spoon them onto the prepared baking sheet, making sure not to crowd. Roast for 25 minutes, giving a shake or a stir halfway through, so potatoes roast evenly.
- Finish with another sprinkle of sea salt and some fresh ground pepper.
- Serves 4. Doubles easily.

Miami Flavors—Momma's Greens—Sukuma Wiki

If you're mystified by what to do with greens in seasonal abundance, this is your recipe. Even if you hate greens, this is your recipe. But really, it's everyone's recipe. I learned a version of it when I taught with Common Threads, the nonprofit empowering kids to cook. It came from a guest chef who learned it from his mother in Jamaica.

Seasonal greens, be they tough end-of-season collards or tender, frilly new kale, are treated with aromatics, spices, and tomatoes. The heat tames the greens, and they wilt right down, softening, and yielding to the bite. Fast and fuss-free, they emerge with a deep color and flavor that's a world away from old-school greens cooked till they're gray and defeated.

I've been making greens this way ever since. But I didn't have a name for it. Neither did the guest chef. They were just his momma's greens. Smart woman, his mom, but I've since learned the recipe isn't hers alone and isn't exclusive to the Caribbean. People have been making it in some form or another all over the world, and why not? It's such an elegant use of a handful of basic ingredients. But it comes from Africa. There it's called sukuma wiki, which means, stretch the week. It's a budget-stretcher for sure, a delicious way to manage your fridge full of greens, and a gift from the African diaspora. Understanding and appreciating its origins makes me love it even more. I've seen kids eat this dish with delight. I hope you will too.

How to serve: Enjoy with Haitian bean gravy (sos pwa) (p. 68) and rice or cornbread.

Ingredients

- 2 tablespoons grapeseed or coconut oil
- 1 large onion, chopped (about 2 cups)
- 2 garlic cloves, minced
- 1 thumb-sized piece of ginger, well-chopped
- 1 teaspoon ground cumin
- 1/2 teaspoon ground coriander
- 1/2 teaspoon ground turmeric
- 2 large tomatoes, coarsely chopped or 1 15-ounce can diced tomatoes
- 1 pound kale, callaloo, collards, or any combination of dark leafy greens, tough stems discarded, well cleaned and coarsely chopped
- 1/2 cup water or vegetable broth
- 2 tablespoons fresh lemon juice
- sea salt and fresh ground pepper to taste
- 1 handful cilantro, chopped (optional)

Instructions

- In a Dutch oven or other large pot, heat oil over medium-high heat. Add the chopped onion and ginger and cook, stirring now and then until they start to soften and turn gold, about 5 minutes. Add minced garlic and cumin, coriander, and turmeric. Continue stirring and cooking for another few minutes or until all the vegetables are gilded in the spiced oil.
- Add tomatoes, all your greens, and water or broth. Mix together well. When the pot starts to simmer, cover, reduce heat to low, and let everybody cook for about 15 minutes until greens are softened and have a flavor that sings of their greenness. If they've thrown off a lot of liquid, continue cooking a few minutes more, stirring occasionally so any excess liquid cooks away.
- Turn off the heat, add lemon juice, and season generously with sea salt and pepper. Sprinkle in chopped cilantro, if using, stir and serve.
- Serves 4. Doubles, even triples. This is your delicious solution to greens overage.

Miami Flavors—Maque Choux

I'd associated maque choux, featuring the Creole holy trinity of onion, pepper, and celery, with New Orleans. But South Florida grows all three as well as three summer besties—tomato, basil, and corn. Maque choux is kin to succotash. They're both corn-centric skillet quick fixes, somewhere between a stew and a sauté, and both have their roots in Native American cuisine. Corn and tomatoes are two of the Magic Eight, the 8 crops Indigenous People gifted to the world (the other 6 - potatoes, beans, squash, chile, vanilla, and the most magic of all, cacao),

How to serve: Ladle up some maque choux. Serve with green salad with tamarind vinaigrette (p. 124) and some crusty bread and the world will feel a little friendlier. A little hot sauce helps, too.

Ingredients

- 2–3 ears corn (about 2 cups)
- 1 tablespoon olive oil
- 1 onion, chopped (about 3/4 cup)
- 1 good-size celery stalk, chopped (about 1/2 cup)
- 1/2 green pepper, chopped (about 1/2 cup)
- 1/2 orange or red pepper, chopped (about 1/2 cup)
- 1/2 jalapeño, minced
- 1 pint grape tomatoes, halved
- 1 teaspoon smoked paprika
- 1 teaspoon fresh thyme leaves (or 1/2 teaspoon dried)
- 1 big handful fresh greens, such as kale, turnip greens or spinach, well-chopped (optional)
- 1 big handful fresh basil, chopped
- sea salt and fresh ground pepper to taste

Instructions

- Working over a large bowl, cut kernels off the corn. Scrape the cobs well, using the bowl to reserve the kernels and any juice from the cobs.
- Heat oil in a skillet, preferably cast iron, over medium-high heat. Add the chopped onion and sauté, stirring occasionally, until the onion starts to soften, about 4 minutes. Then add the celery and pepper. Continue cooking and stirring until vegetables grow soft and fragrant, about another 5 minutes.
- Stir in the jalapeño, grape tomatoes, corn, thyme, and smoked paprika. Reduce heat to medium, cover, and let the maque choux simmer for 10 minutes. Mixture will throw off liquid, creating its own broth.
- Remove lid, add optional chopped greens, and stir until greens just wilt. Add chopped fresh basil and season generously with sea salt and fresh ground pepper.
- Serves 4.

Miami Flavors—Sofkee (Okay, call 'em grits)

Maybe you call cornmeal mush grits. Maybe you call it polenta. Maybe you call it mamaliga as they do in Romania. For many indigenous tribes, including Florida's Seminole and Miccosukee, it's sofkee, and they should get dibs on the name. They were growing, drying, and grinding corn millennia before Columbus even got here. Sofkee was both a staple of their diet and something served to honored guests.

Traditionally, this pot of creamy comfort involves dried ground corn, a lot of water, and a whole lot of time stirring and standing over an open fire or at the stove. There's a better way. Baking—no splatters, no stirring. Granted, it's not pretty when it goes in the oven, still not a knockout when it first comes out, but give it a stir, add sea salt and pepper, and it all comes together for a pot of wow, something greater than the sum of its parts.

How to serve: Sofkee has a million applications. It can be rich and pourable, it can be firm, it can be chilled, then sliced and roasted or fried so the slices become crispy cakes (p. 134).

Make it richer with a pat or three of vegan butter or drizzle on some cashew cream. Make it cheesier by adding nutritional yeast and/or grated vegan cheese. Add a fistful of your favorite herbs, chopped tomato, and/or chopped jalapeño. Let sofkee serve as a plush bed for grilled or roasted vegetables, sukuma wiki (p. 128), Cuban black beans (p. 88), or mushroom étouffée (p. 75). Or do as the Seminole do, and enjoy sofkee's sweeter side—top with fresh fruit, cinnamon, chopped nuts, and a drizzle of cashew cream or molasses.

Ingredients

- 2 tablespoons olive oil
- 4–5 cups water—4 for a thicker, oomphier sofkee, 5 for a softer, creamier sofkee
- 1 cup medium or coarse cornmeal, sometimes labeled as polenta
- sea salt and fresh ground pepper—be generous

Instructions

- Preheat oven to 350°F.
- Gently oil a deep ovenproof casserole. Pour in water, then the cornmeal. Give a stir so it forms a slurry. It will not look pretty. Take heart.
- Place the casserole uncovered in the oven for an hour. Give sofkee a vigorous stir so it's smooth and lumpless. If it hasn't thickened enough to your liking, return it to the oven for another 10–15 minutes. Give it another stir, then season lavishly.
- Serves 4 to 6.

Miami Flavors— Crispy Grits Cakes

Creaminess has a lot going for it. But so does crispiness. Grits can do it all.

How to serve: Enjoy them crispy and corny all by themselves, or top with tomato choka (p. 48), serve with chimichurri (p. 123), or pair with momma's greens (p. 128).

Ingredients

- 1 cup of cornmeal
- 4 cups of water
- sea salt

Instructions

- Prepare and bake for 1 hour as per sofkee recipe (p. 132). Stir, season, and allow to cool slightly.
- Lightly oil an 8 × 8-inch baking pan or layer cake pan.
- Pour in sofkee, cover, and refrigerate for 6 hours or even overnight, until grits condense and become firm.
- Turn out and slice as desired, such as rounds, batons, wedges, or triangles.
- Preheat oven to 400°F. Line a rimmed baking sheet with parchment paper or a Silpat.
- Gently place grits cakes on the baking sheet. Brush them lightly with olive oil and sprinkle with sea salt.
- Bake for 15–20 minutes or until the edges are lightly blackened. Flip grits cakes gently and bake for another 10 minutes or until they're golden and crispy.
- Serves 4 to 6.

Miami Favorites—Two Fish-Free Caviars

Miami Flavors—Cowboy Caviar

Cowboys started in Florida. So did cows. It's a fact. The country's first cows came to the New World from the Old World. Some credit Columbus, some credit Ponce de Leon, but either way, cows sailed over here from Spain. That must have been a tough trip for a bovine.

Cowboy caviar, however, comes from Texas, created, according to legend, by the director of Neiman Marcus restaurants. Cowboy caviar contains no cow, no caviar. It's vegan and always has been, with beans, corn, and peppers, traditionally dressed with a little vinegar and sugar, for a sweet-sour kind of deal. It's sorta salad, sorta salsa, with a gentle joke of a name—not too many cows or cowboys shop at Neiman Marcus. Dialing up the lime juice and adding pigeon peas and allspice makes it Miami.

How to serve: Make cowboy caviar ahead and keep it covered and refrigerated letting the dressing infuse the ingredients. Cowboy caviar is a happy addition to a picnic, potluck, buffet, or tailgate. It won't wilt or turn soggy. Serve with flatbread.

For a fun party presentation, just before serving, split a Florida avocado and remove the pit. Stuff the well with cowboy caviar. Sprinkle a little lime juice on the exposed avocado halves to keep them looking fresh.

Ingredients

For the dressing:
- 3 tablespoons olive oil
- 1 tablespoon red wine vinegar
- 3 tablespoons fresh lime juice
- 1 teaspoon cane sugar
- 1 teaspoon cumin
- 1/2 teaspoon allspice

For the caviar:
- 2 cups black-eyed peas, cooked and cooled
- 2 cups pigeon peas or black beans, cooked and cooled
- 2 ears corn (about 1-1/2 cups)
- 1 red pepper, diced (about 1 cup)
- 1 jalapeño, minced
- 1 ripe tomato or 1/2 pint grape tomatoes, diced
- 1/2 cup mild onion, like Vidalia, sliced, or 1/2 cup thinly sliced scallions
- sea salt and fresh ground pepper
- 1 handful cilantro leaves, chopped

Instructions

- In a small bowl, pour in the olive oil, red wine vinegar, lime juice, cane sugar, cumin, and allspice. Whisk together for a minute or two or until sugar dissolves and dressing emulsifies. Set aside.
- In a large bowl, combine black-eyed peas and pigeon peas (or black beans), corn, sweet pepper, jalapeño, tomato, and onion. Give a good stir, so everything's mixed together.
- Pour dressing over the beans and corn mixture and stir again. Season generously with sea salt and pepper. Recipe can be made up to a day ahead and kept covered and refrigerated at this point.
- Just before serving, add the cilantro, taste again for salt, toss again, and serve.
- Serves 4 to 6.

Miami Flavors—Eggplant Caviar

Eggplant is one of the few vegetables that can survive Miami summer heat. It loves grill and kitchen heat too, its flesh turning melty and tender and endlessly adaptable—Provençal ratatouille, Italian caponata, Balkan avjar, Middle Eastern baba ghanoush, sweet and spicy Szechuan eggplant, sultry Indian baingan bharta, Moroccan candied eggplant, twin of the classic Spanish tapa, honey-glazed eggplant, and Turkish imam bayaldi, slow-roasted stuffed eggplant which means the imam fainted with pleasure.

You could go around the world eating eggplant, fainting with pleasure, and many of these dishes—not quite salad, not quite dip—overlap with many iterations, many names, including eggplant caviar, claimed from St. Petersburg, Russia to St. Petersburg, Florida.

Don't worry, there's no fish, no eggs, or fish eggs in this caviar. The name comes from eggplant's tiny seeds, and the fact that it tastes lavish but is far more affordable than that strange, salty, fishy stuff. The taste may sing Middle Eastern to you. That's the allspice.

How to serve: Serve over greens with whole grain pita or sesame-studded crackers for scooping, or as a sandwich filling. I like it at room temperature, but it's also good chilled. Can be made ahead, during which time flavors magically deepen and improve.

Ingredients

- 2 tablespoons olive oil
- 1 eggplant, diced (about 2 cups)
- 3 cloves garlic, chopped
- 1 onion, chopped (about 1 cup)
- 1 jalapeño, chopped
- 1 15-ounce can diced tomatoes
- 1 tablespoon tomato paste
- 1 teaspoon allspice
- sea salt to taste
- juice of 1/2 lemon
- 1 handful flat-leaf parsley, chopped
- optional—1 handful toasted pine nuts for garnish

Instructions

- Heat oil in a large skillet over medium-high heat. Add eggplant, garlic, onion, and jalapeño, and cook, stirring until vegetables soften, about 8–10 minutes.
- Add tomatoes, tomato paste, and allspice. Bring to a simmer, then reduce heat to medium. Keep cooking, stirring occasionally, for 20 minutes or until the vegetables are very tender and the tomatoes have thickened. Recipe may be made several days ahead and kept covered and chilled.
- Just before serving, squeeze on the lemon and taste again, adding more sea salt if desired. Sprinkle on chopped parsley and optional pine nuts.
- Serves 4 to 6.

Miami Favorites—House-Smoked Tempeh

Tempeh is a fabulous fermented soybean cake. Indonesian in origin, it dates to the 16th century. Despite its history, many people still don't know what to do with it. But what if you could make it taste like bacon? You can. House-smoked tempeh keeps bacon's salty, smoky flavor and a little fattiness without the saturated fat and without the pigs, who are just as smart and adorable as you are. The process is quick and easy, involving no smoker, and gives you a little tempeh fermentation wattage, too.

How to serve: Enjoy as a side with scrambled tofu (p. 9), top collard tacos (p. 105) with it, add to Cuban rice with jackfruit (p. 78), and any dish where you want to bump up the flavor and appeal. Much easier and tidier to cook than bacon.

For a more tropical note, baste with mango barbecue sauce (p. 118) instead of the smoky miso paste.

Ingredients

- 2 tablespoons shiro miso (white miso)
- 2 tablespoons agave
- 2 teaspoons liquid smoke
- 1 teaspoon smoked paprika
- 1 tablespoon grapeseed or other neutral oil, divided use
- 1 8-ounce package tempeh, sliced into thin strips
- 1/3 cup water

Instructions

- In a small bowl, combine the miso, agave liquid smoke, and smoked paprika with 2 teaspoons olive oil. Stir briefly until it forms a smooth but thickish paste.
- Lay tempeh strips on a plate.
- Using a pastry brush, paint the smoky miso paste on the tempeh.
- Set a skillet, preferably cast iron, on a burner and heat the remaining tablespoon of oil over medium-high heat. When the oil starts to shimmer, add your painted tempeh strips, spreading them out so they're not too crowded. Now pour the water over all. It'll look soupy at first but will reduce as the tempeh cooks.
- After about 5 minutes, flip the tempeh and continue to cook for another 3–5 minutes or until your tempeh darkens, turns appealingly sticky, and the liquid has cooked away, leaving only the flavor.
- Serves 3 to 4.

Miami Flavors—Coconut Green Beans

This is essentially a stir-fry, a quick-cook dish with a balance of sweet, salty, zingy, and munchy. Neither tamarind nor coconut (which can be a very pushy flavor) dominate. They play well together. The ease of this recipe invites you to try with different vegetables. I've made it with eggplant, zucchini, and probably something else I've forgotten, but I think green beans are best. They keep their shape and bright flavor. They deliver a nice amount of vitamin C and folate, too.

How to serve: Enjoy this dry-ish India-inspired dish with brown rice studded with a few toasted cumin seeds, and a good soupy dal.

To make this kid-friendly, keep the tamarind and coconut, and lose the warming notes of turmeric, cumin, and hing.

For a slightly different presentation, give the green beans a fine chop, so the bits are pea-sized. In India, it's called a thoran. It's a quick and winning recipe, however you slice it. Pardon the pun.

Ingredients

- 1 pound green beans, trimmed
- 2 teaspoons tamarind paste (or secret substitute p. 124)
- 1 tablespoon coconut oil or grapeseed oil
- 3 tablespoons dried unsweetened coconut flakes
- 1 tablespoon fresh ginger, minced
- 1 tablespoon chickpea flour (aka besan)
- 1/4 teaspoon turmeric
- 1/2 teaspoon cumin
- pinch hing (aka asafoetida or devil's dung), optional*
- pinch of sea salt, plus more to taste
- a few curry leaves, if you've got 'em**
- handful chopped cilantro to finish

Instructions

- Steam green beans for 3–4 minutes, so they're still bright green and crisp. Set aside to cool.
- In a small saucepan, combine tamarind paste with 1 tablespoon water. Stir until tamarind dissolves, and in 3–4 minutes, you have a thickish, murky sauce.
- In a small bowl, mix together the chickpea flour, turmeric, cumin, optional hing, and sea salt. Set aside.
- In a large skillet, heat the oil over medium-high heat, until it starts to shimmer. Add coconut and ginger. Stir, until coconut flakes turn golden and ginger softens and turns fragrant, about 3–5 minutes. Keep stirring to prevent coconut from burning.
- Add the green beans and chickpea-spice mixture and toss to combine.
- Reduce heat to medium. Pour tamarind sauce over all and toss again. Add curry leaves, if available, and continue cooking until green beans are crisp-tender and well-coated with the coconut and spice mixture.
- Season with sea salt and finish with chopped cilantro.
- Serves 4.

---

* Hing, asafoetida, and devil's dung are three different names for the same aromatic (some would say smelly) resin. Usually available dried and powdered, it smells strong in the bottle but mellows in cooking, adding allium-like funk and umami to dishes. Often used when cooking beans to make them more digestible.

Plantains

Miami loves plantains. This beloved fruit, which sometimes acts like a vegetable, originated in Southeast Asia but thrives in the Caribbean, Latin America, and South Florida. Plantains look like bananas, but are bigger, starchier, and thicker-skinned. They're picked when they're green-skinned and underripe, which is how many people love them best. So what do you do with an unripe plantain? Make tostones! Or as they call them in Haiti, bannann peze.

In any language, making tostones takes but 3 ingredients—green plantains, oil, and salt. Simple! Or so you'd think. Preparation involves peeling your plantains, boiling to tenderize, slicing, deep-frying, smashing, and then frying them again. Not simple, not tidy, but when done right, they offer a wow of crispiness. Think of them like a cross between potato chips and French fries, with a little Latin/Caribbean flavor of their own. No wonder people love them. The good news is you'll find tostones in almost every Latin and Caribbean eatery in Miami.

You'll also find platanos maduros on the menu in the same Miami restaurants, but you'll find them in my kitchen too. Platanos maduros, or ripe plantains, are the same fruit, but another story. They're much quicker and easier to make, with less mess and fuss, and offer a very different tasting experience. They're meltingly tender, and with ripeness comes sweetness. For proper platanos maduros, plantains should be beyond speckly, they should be black-skinned, more like something you'd think to throw out rather than want to eat. Their beauty reveals itself when you taste them.

Miami Favorites—Ripe Sweet Plantains—Platanos Maduros

Many restaurants serve plantains so they're melting and gleaming with butter. Here, less is more. This recipe takes you from plantain to plate in 15 minutes, no muss, no fuss.

How to serve: The classic Cuban pairing is to serve them with black beans (p. 88) or picadillo (p. 80).

Ingredients

- 2 teaspoons vegan butter
- 2 very ripe plantains
- 1 teaspoon evaporated cane sugar or coconut sugar
- pinch cayenne
- pinch sea salt
- juice of 1 lime

Instructions

- Heat butter in a skillet, preferably cast iron, over medium-high heat.
- Peel plantains and slice diagonally into 1/2-inch slices.
- When butter is melted and bubbly, add the plantain slices, allowing space between them so there's no crowding.
- In a small bowl or ramekin, mix together sugar, cayenne, and sea salt. Sprinkle over the plantain slices.
- Cook for about 5 minutes or until plantain slices soften and turn golden brown at the edges. Flip gently and cook for another 3–5 minutes or until they're burnished and tender.
- Squeeze lime juice over all and serve at once.
- Serves 4. Recipe doubles easily, and everybody loves them.

Azucar! Miami Celebrates Sweetness

Azucar!

Miami has a sweet tooth. Lucky for us, we're situated just southeast of the nation's sweet spot for sugar production, Palm Beach County's broad swath of rich-soiled farmland. Florida sugar is close to a $5 billion industry. But it's not about money, it's about love. We start the day with a shot of sugar-laced cafecito and keep it going with tropical fruits, which despite their refreshing zing are deceptively high in sugar, and Caribbean and Latin desserts that aren't shy on sweetness. We love it so much, the Spanish word for sugar, azucar, was the catchphrase of exuberant Celia Cruz, the queen of salsa. These desserts are designed to make you throw back your head and shout Azucar! like you mean it.

Miami Favorites—Iced Cafecito

Cafecito culture is so intrinsic to Miami life, it can even show up as dessert. At least it can here. The texture of this dessert is light, airy, and mousse-y, but the flavor—coffee married to chocolate—is dark and decadent. The recipe calls for 1 tablespoon of espresso powder, the same kind you'd use for Cuban coffee (p. 4). For caffeine-sensitive folks who don't want the all-night jitters, look for caffeine-free espresso powder.

How to serve: Iced cafecito needs to chill for several hours before serving. That means it's a do-ahead perfect for parties. Spoon it into demitasses, coffee cups, or a pretty serving bowl. Serve it with coconut shortbread (p. 149) and it'll scream Miami.

Ingredients

- 6 ounces dark chocolate (70% cacao)
- 3/4 cup aquafaba
- 1/4 teaspoon cream of tartar
- 1/2 cup evaporated cane sugar
- 1 tablespoon finely ground espresso powder
- 1 teaspoon vanilla, Kahlua, or rum

Instructions

- In a small saucepan, slowly melt chocolate over low heat. Add espresso powder and stir until dissolved. Set aside and allow to cool.
- In a standing mixer, whip the aquafaba and cream of tartar on high for a really long time—up to 10 minutes or until the aquafaba is billowy, fills the bowl, and stands in fairly stiff peaks.
- Once the chocolate cools to room temperature, stir in flavoring—vanilla, Kahlua or rum—and fold into the aquafaba, keeping a very light hand.
- Pour into demitasses, coffee cups, or a pretty serving bowl, and refrigerate for at least 4 hours.
- Serves 6 to 8.

Miami Flavors—Coconut Shortbread

These shortbread cookies are buttery but butterless, mildly sweet, and coconutty. You can up the coconut flavor by substituting coconut extract for the vanilla.

How to serve: A wedge of coconut shortbread is nice with tea or café Cubano (p. 4), but serve it with iced cafecito (p. 147) or magic mango mousse (p. 150) and taste Miami.

Ingredients

- 1/2 cup dried shredded coconut flakes, unsweetened
- 8 tablespoons vegan butter (1 stick)
- 4 tablespoons (1/4 cup) coconut oil
- 1/2 cup evaporated cane sugar
- pinch sea salt
- 1/2 teaspoon vanilla
- 1-1/3 cup unbleached all-purpose flour
- optional—1 tablespoon demerara sugar to finish

Instructions

- Preheat oven to 325°F. Spread coconut on a rimmed baking sheet. Bake until coconut is light golden, stirring occasionally, about 8 minutes. Set aside briefly to cool.
- Using an electric mixer; beat vegan butter, coconut oil, and sugar in a large bowl, just until pale and creamy. Mix in salt and vanilla. Beat in flour in 2 additions. Stir in toasted coconut.
- Gather dough together, flatten it into a disc, and wrap well in plastic. Refrigerate for at least 1 hour or up to 2 days. Soften slightly at room temperature before rolling out.
- Preheat oven to 300°F.
- Line a rimmed baking sheet with parchment paper.
- Roll out dough disc between two sheets of lightly floured parchment so it forms a 9-inch round about 1/4-inch thick. Carefully return the dough to the fridge for another 30 minutes to firm up.
- Gently place the dough on the prepared baking sheet. With a chef's knife, lightly cut the disc into 16 skinny wedges, taking care not to cut all the way through. Lightly prick the shortbread with a fork and sprinkle on demerara sugar if desired.
- Place the baking sheet in the middle oven rack and bake for 30 minutes. Cookies will be pale and slightly soft right out of the oven. They firm up as they cool.
- Slice into wedges while still warm (about 10 minutes or so), using the knife lines drawn earlier as a guide. They should separate easily.
- Makes 16.

Miami Flavors—Magic Mango Mousse

Eating a fresh mango can be a deliciously messy affair. I've stained more than one shirt with vibrant orange mango juice. Magic mango mousse gives you all the mango flavor and fun in a tidier, fluffier format, with puréed mango suspended in a cloud of aquafaba meringue.

Refrigerate for a few hours before serving, and you and the mousse will be all set—magic!

How to serve: Serve in pretty dessert cups, garnishing with a little diced mango and a few mint leaves.

Ingredients

- 1/2 cup aquafaba
- 1/2 teaspoon cream of tartar
- 1 cup sweetened condensed coconut milk
- 2 cups mango purée, from about 2 ripe mangos, or use frozen, thawed mango
- 1 teaspoon rum or vanilla
- 1 teaspoon lime juice
- optional garnish:
- a little extra diced mango
- a few mint leaves

Instructions

- Whip aquafaba and cream of tartar in a standing mixer. I mean whip the dickens out of it, until the aquafaba stands in stiff peaks like meringue. This may take up to 10 minutes.
- Spoon the whipped aquafaba into a separate bowl and pop in the fridge to keep it cool and light.
- Now whip together the mango, sweetened condensed coconut milk, rum and lime juice for a minute or two, just until smooth.
- Gently fold the aquafaba into the mango mixture and voila, you have magic mango mousse. Spoon into dessert cups and let chill for at least an hour.
- Serves 4 to 6.

Miami Flavors—Sunshine Squares with Chocolate Chunks

Buttery, chewy, chocolate studded with a whisper of orange, these bars are just the ticket when you want a bite of something sweet. If you're more into cakey bars, stir 1/3 cup unsweetened applesauce into the melted butter and sugar, and proceed with the recipe as written.

How to serve: Enjoy as an after-school treat, make a batch to impress your new neighbors. Dust with powdered sugar or drizzle on the chocolate orange glaze (p. 170) for a stylish finish.

Ingredients

- 8 tablespoons vegan butter (1 stick)
- 1/2 cup brown sugar, lightly packed
- 1/3 cup evaporated cane sugar
- 2 tablespoons aquafaba
- 1/4 cup fresh orange juice
- 1 teaspoon Grand Marnier or other orange liqueur (optional)
- 1-1/3 cups unbleached all-purpose flour
- 1/2 teaspoon baking soda
- 1/2 teaspoon ground cinnamon
- zest of 1 orange
- 1 3-1/2 ounce bar bittersweet chocolate, coarsely chopped (about 1/2 cup)

Instructions

- Preheat oven to 350°F. Lightly oil an 8 × 8-inch baking pan.
- In a medium-sized bowl, sift together flour, baking soda, and cinnamon. Grate in orange zest. Stir to combine and set aside.
- In a saucepan over medium heat, melt the butter. Pour in the brown sugar and evaporated cane sugar. Stir until sugar dissolves.
- Add the aquafaba, fresh orange juice, and optional Grand Marnier. Stir again to combine.
- Slowly pour the flour mixture into the melted butter mixture, stirring just until it comes together as a batter.
- Pour the batter into the prepared pan, smooth the top, and scatter on the chopped chocolate.
- Bake until the bars are golden brown and set, 30 minutes.
- Remove from oven and let cool completely before slicing into squares.
- Makes 16 squares.

Miami Flavors—Orange-Scented Almond Cookies

I cannot tell a lie—these orange-scented cookies owe more to Tuscany than Miami, but they're easy, tender, chewy, and melt in the mouth. They're like the love child of meringue and amaretti.

How to serve: Store in an airtight tin and enjoy within 3 days—Miami humidity does them no favors—or freeze them, and they'll keep for months.

Ingredients

- 2-1/2 cups blanched almond flour
- 1-1/2 cups powdered sugar, plus more for finishing cookies
- grated zest of 1 orange
- 1/2 teaspoon almond extract or Grand Marnier or other orange liqueur
- 1/4 cup aquafaba
- 1/8 teaspoon cream of tartar

Instructions

- In a large bowl, sift together all the almond flour and 1-1/2 cups powdered sugar. Add the grated orange zest and stir so the mixture is light and well combined.
- Pour aquafaba into a standing mixer. Sprinkle in the cream of tartar and whip on the highest setting until the aquafaba is thick and billowy—about 5–7 minutes. Add almond extract or orange liqueur and continue to whip for another few minutes, until the aquafaba is glossy and stands up in peaks.
- Fold the almond flour thoroughly into the aquafaba to form the cookie dough. Gather up the dough and flatten it slightly into a disc. Wrap well in plastic wrap and refrigerate for at least 12 hours or up to 3 days. During that time, that little bit of orange zest wafts through the cookie dough and adds bright flavor
- Preheat oven to 325°F.
- Line two rimmed baking sheets with parchment paper. Sprinkle a handful of powdered sugar on a clean work surface. Remove the dough from the fridge. Use your hands to roll the dough out into a long, slender log, about 1 inch in diameter. Slice the dough into about 2 dozen 1/2-inch rounds. Place on baking sheets, spreading cooking about 2 inches apart. Wet your hands with water, then with damp hands flatten the cookies slightly to form ovals.
- Give the cookies a good dusting of powdered sugar, then bake for 20 minutes.
- Cookies will be pale, with a few crackles on top. They'll be very soft right out of the oven, but firm up beautifully as they cool. Let them sit on the baking sheets for 10–15 minutes then gently remove to a cooling rack or plate and let them continue to rest and cool for 1 hour.
- Makes 2 dozen.

Miami Flavors—Triple Gingerbread

Gingerbread evokes chilly New England nights—or Hansel and Gretel, who ate the witch's house with unfortunate results. But ginger is a tropical rhizome (not a root, a rhizome) so heat-tolerant and hearty, even I can grow it. Fresh ginger is used all over the Caribbean to punch up flavor, and it's in this gingerbread, along with powdered ginger and crystallized ginger.

I do not peel fresh ginger, but if you want to fuss, peel the brown skin away with a paring knife. Some people swear using the edge of a spoon works well, too. Good on them.

The correct name for a harvested clump or cluster of ginger is a hand. Fresh ginger should be firm—not woody, not mushy—fragrant and a little juicy. Older ginger dries out and gets fibrous. I suppose the same thing happens with humans. But let's not go there, let's enjoy the moment and enjoy the gingerbread. It's magically light in texture, bright in taste, and swings tropical and not so much Grimm's fairy tales. It leaves the meh gingerbreads you've had (come on, you know you have) in the dust.

How to serve: Gingerbread is best at room temperature.

Ingredients

- 2 cups unbleached all-purpose flour
- 1/4 cup whole wheat flour
- 1-1/2 teaspoon baking soda
- 2 teaspoons cinnamon
- 2 teaspoon ginger
- 1 teaspoon allspice
- 1 teaspoon nutmeg
- 1/2 teaspoon clove
- 1/2 cup grapeseed or other neutral oil
- 1/2 cup evaporated cane sugar
- 1 cup molasses
- 1 cup coffee, hot
- 1/2 cup unsweetened applesauce
- 1 tablespoon fresh ginger, minced
- 1/3 cup crystallized ginger, chopped, plus more for decorating. if desired

Instructions

- Preheat oven to 350°F.
- Oil a 10-cup bundt pan, making sure all the crannies get lubed. Give it a light dusting of flour and knock out any excess.
- In a large bowl, sift together unbleached flour, whole wheat flour, baking soda, and dried spices.
- In a separate bowl, whisk oil, sugar, molasses, coffee, and applesauce until thick and well-combined.
- Add wet ingredients to dry and stir just until you have a thick, dark, fragrant batter. Then gently add the fresh and crystallized ginger and give one more stir.
- Pour batter into the prepared pan and bake for 40 minutes or until gingerbread puffs, smells like a fairytale fantasy, and springs back when gently prodded with a finger.
- Allow cake to cool completely; then gently unmold.
- Dust with powdered sugar or finish with a powdered sugar glaze—2 cups sifted powdered sugar mixed with 2–3 tablespoons lemon juice or plant-based milk and stirred until smooth and satiny. Drizzle all over the cake and give the glaze a few minutes to set. Maybe scatter some chopped crystallized ginger on top for sparkle, Or play up the Caribbean accent with a dollop of whipped coconut cream (recipe p. 165).
- Serves 8 to 10.

 **Starfruit**

"And so we came forth and once again beheld the stars." —Dante Alighieri, *The Inferno*

Miami's neon lights edge out the stars at night, but we have stars within easy reach—starfruit, aka carambola. Originally from Southeast Asia, carambola has been cultivated here for over a century. From mid-winter through summer, the fruit dangles from trees like magic lantern ornaments.

A whole fruit is about as long as your hand, yellow, oblong, and pentagonal. Sliced crosswise, though, and you see stars. Wincingly tart when greenish, allow the carambola to ripen till its skin is sunshine yellow with brown beginning at the tips. Bring one to your nose. It should bear a light, floral fragrance, like a spritz of orange blossom water. The fruit's flavor is mild, with a whisper of grape, but really glams up a dish . A few slices make a green salad pop. It's delicious with a sprinkle of magic dust (p. 39), but a little tricky to bake with. Don't worry, I've got you covered.

Miami Favorites—All-Star Upside Down Cake

Starfruit in an upside-down cake seems like a meant-to-be. Switch out the usual pineapple for carambola, invert, golden stars on top, and voila—natural food styling! You'd think.

I'll tell you something others won't—starfruit, with its mild apple-to-grape flavor, is less juicy, less sweet, and more astringent than pineapple. So while a starfruit upside-down cake looks knockout, the cake can be on the dry side, and the delightful sugary, buttery business we love in an upside-down cake may be lacking.

Keep the upside-down concept, add a few slices of starfruit for looks if you like, but this upside-down cake lets any seasonal fruit star. I've made it with berries in the spring, mango in the summer, apples in the fall, and last season's frozen berries in the winter. It's a year-round win.

How to serve: Serve warm, with whipped coconut cream, if you like (recipe p. 165).

Ingredients

- 10 tablespoons vegan butter, divided use
- 1/2 cup brown sugar
- 2 cups fresh fruit (or frozen and thawed) sliced into 1/2-inch pieces (berries can be left whole)
- 1/2 cup evaporated cane sugar
- 1/2 cup applesauce
- 1/3 cup plain unsweetened vegan yogurt
- 2 tablespoons rum,* divided use
- 2 cups unbleached all-purpose flour
- 2 teaspoons baking powder

Instructions

- Preheat oven to 350°F. Melt 4 tablespoons of vegan butter in a 9-inch cast iron skillet or cake pan. Sprinkle brown sugar evenly on top.
- Slice mangoes, plums, starfruit, or your fruit of choice into 1/2-inch pieces. Berries can be left whole.
- Channel your inner artist. Arrange fruit on top, covering as much surface as you can. Spoon one tablespoon of rum over all. Set aside.
- In a large bowl, sift together the flour and baking powder.
- In a saucepan over medium heat, melt the remaining 6 tablespoons of vegan butter. Add the evaporated cane sugar and stir until the sugar dissolves. Remove from the burner,

---

* If you prefer to omit alcohol, substitute orange juice.

spoon in the applesauce, vegan yogurt, and the other tablespoon of rum. Give another stir to combine.
- Stir into the flour mixture, blending only until it comes together for a thick, smooth batter.
- Spoon batter over the fruit, covering thoroughly.
- Bake for 30–40 minutes or until the top (it's actually the bottom once you invert the cake) is golden brown and a toothpick or other tester inserted in the center comes out clean—no crumbs.
- Allow the cake to cool for 10 minutes, then run a knife around the edges to free the cake and invert onto a cake plate.
- Serves 6 to 8.

Miami Favorites—Summer Fruit Cobbler

Summer in Miami means mangos and blueberries. It may mean peaches, cherries, and plums for you. Be it stone fruit or berries, a cobbler's what you need to show off your local summer bounty. That's a cobbler, as in cobbled together. Cobblers are made for summer. They're more forgiving and less demanding than baking a pie and still enhance fresh fruit with butter, sugar, and heat. It's also a great vehicle for that farmer's market haul of fresh fruit you haven't gotten around to eating.

Some cobbler recipes call for biscuit dough. This cobbler recipe, made with a batter, involves no rolling of dough—the batter's on the bottom, the fruit goes on the top, and it goes into the oven, bing, bang, boom. Like I said, cobblers seem made for summer.

How to serve: Add a blob of whipped coconut cream (p. 165) if you like. I just like it as it is, warm from the oven.

Ingredients

- 8 tablespoons vegan butter (1 stick)
- 3/4 cup unbleached all-purpose flour
- 2 teaspoons baking powder
- 1 cup evaporated cane sugar
- 3/4 cup unsweetened oat milk
- 3 cups fresh fruit, sliced (berries can be left whole)

Instructions

- Preheat oven to 350°F. Melt vegan butter in a 6-cup casserole or 8 × 8-inch baking dish.
- In a medium bowl, mix together the flour, baking powder and sugar. Pour in the oat milk and stir until smooth.
- Carefully pour about half of the melted butter into the batter, leaving the rest in the baking dish. Stir the batter together to incorporate, then pour it into the baking dish.
- Spoon the fruit on top, keeping it mostly toward the center. As the cobbler bakes, the batter will rise up to cradle and encase the fruit.
- Bake the cobbler for 1 hour or until a tester inserted in the batter comes out clean. Allow to cool slightly
- Serves 6.

Miami Flavors—Strawberry Kuchen

Kuchen, German for cake, belongs to the family of cobblers, slumps, grunts, buckles, sonkers, betties, and all those homey fruit and batter desserts with unlovely names. There's no sweet spice, no fancy liqueur, and no need for them. The flavor is pure strawberry. If you don't have almond flour or have a nut allergy, this works quite well using only unbleached all-purpose flour. It's so easy, you can make it up before a meal, bake, then have it ready for dessert.

Adapted with gratitude from a recipe by *Black Girl Baking* author Jerrelle Guy.

How to serve: Best served fresh, still warm from the oven. Garnish with a dusting of powdered sugar or with a dollop of whipped coconut cream (p. 165).

Ingredients

- 8 tablespoons vegan butter (1 stick), melted and cooled slightly
- 1 cup fresh or frozen and thawed strawberries, sliced if large
- 2/3 cup brown sugar, packed
- 1/2 cup plant-based milk of your choice—oat and almond are proven winners here
- 2/3 cup unbleached all-purpose flour
- 1/3 cup almond flour
- 1 teaspoon baking powder

Instructions

- Preheat oven to 350°F. Lightly oil an 8-inch cake pan.
- Take out 3 medium-sized bowls without getting annoyed. Strawberries are sensitive and pick up on bad vibes. So do I.
- Pour berries into Bowl #1. Pour in 1/3 cup brown sugar, reserving the remaining 1/3 cup for the cake batter. Stir together berries and sugar and set aside.
- In Bowl #2, whisk together melted vegan butter, plant-based milk, and the rest of the brown sugar. Stir briefly until sugar dissolves.
- In Bowl #3, sift together unbleached all-purpose flour, almond flour, and baking powder. Pour in the contents of Bowl #2. Stir lightly until batter is smooth and well combined.
- Pour batter into the cake pan, spreading so it covers the bottom completely. Scatter berries and their juice from Bowl #1 on top.
- Bake for 25 minutes or until cake smells mmmmm like melted butter and strawberry jam, and top is golden, puffed, and springs back when given a gentle poke.
- Serves 4 to 6.

Miami Flavors—Strawberry Pudding

Here's another simple strawberry recipe with some history behind it, and a few extra names. It's English in origin, as a good many puddings are, and was spa cuisine before anyone knew the term. The Brits once called it hydropathic pudding but the name didn't test market well. It's also called summer pudding, but Miami's strawberries are ripe and ready in the winter. Yeah, we're screwy.

By any name, it's easy, made with 4 simple ingredients - berries, sugar, orange juice, and bread. Save your fancy brioche or crusty artisanal loaf for another day. Plain white or whole wheat bread, the squishy supermarket kind, is what's called for here.

How to serve: Strawberry pudding is naturally fat-free, which is nice, but I've got nothing against fat. Feel free to top it with a dollop of whipped coconut cream (p. 165).

Ingredients

- 1/3 cup orange juice
- 1/2 cup evaporated cane sugar
- 5 cups strawberries (or any mix of fresh blueberries, strawberries, raspberries, blackberries)
- half a loaf of soft white or whole wheat bread (about 15 slices), crusts removed

Instructions

- Lightly oil a 9 × 5-inch loaf pan or 6-cup mold or pudding basin (to use the delightfully archaic British term).
- Warm orange juice and sugar in a large pot or saucepan over medium heat. Stir for a minute or two, until sugar dissolves. Pour in all your berries. Stir and continue cooking until the berries break down a little and release all their lovely juice, about 5 minutes. Remove from heat.
- Ladle a generous amount of vibrant red berry juice—not the berries themselves—enough to cover the bottom of the loaf pan or pudding mold. Top berry juice with a layer of bread, cutting slices to fit. Line the sides of the mold with bread sliced snugly to fit, as well.
- Now layer on a good third of your strawberries, so they completely bury the bread beneath. Top the berries with another layer of bread. Repeat with another layer of strawberries and juice, then top with another layer of bread. Save the last third of the strawberries and juice to cover the top, making sure there's no bread peeking through.
- When the pudding is completely cooled, press a layer or two of plastic wrap on top, then weigh it down by setting a heavy plate or something similar on top. Innovate. I've used an eggplant that happened to be right there in the fridge and that worked fine.

- Refrigerate. Let the strawberries and bread smoosh and the pudding chill overnight or up to two days.
- When you're ready to serve, remove weight, take the pudding from the fridge, and unwrap. Run a knife around the edge and cover the pudding with a plate with a lip (to save any juice) or a shallow bowl. Invert the pudding onto the plate. It should unmold perfectly.
- Stop, admire, then serve, cutting into wedges or slices as desired.
- Serves 6.

Miami Flavors—Whipped Coconut Cream

Whipped coconut cream is fluffy, opulent, and easy. It takes but 3 ingredients and a few steps, but requires a little planning. The coconut milk or cream must be full-fat and must chill overnight first to allow the rich fat coconut cream to rise to the top. Chilling the mixing bowl and beaters for 30 minutes prior to making the whipped cream helps too. Don't shake or tip the can, or you'll undo all that coconut goodness.

Ingredients

- 1 15-ounce can full-fat coconut milk
- 1/2 cup powdered sugar, or more if desired
- 1/2 teaspoon vanilla

Instructions

- Chill the coconut milk or cream on the top shelf of your refrigerator overnight. When you're ready to whip, gently open the can without tipping or shaking it, and spoon the thick coconut cream into the chilled bowl of a standing mixer. Reserve the thinner coconut milk left in the can for another use.
- Whip the cream at medium speed, working up to the highest speed until it's thick and luscious. Pour in the powdered sugar and vanilla extract, then whip again until well combined. If you want it sweeter, add another 2 tablespoons of powdered sugar, whip, then taste again for sweetness. Enjoy right away or keep tightly covered and chilled.
- Makes 2 cups.

 # Cacao

There's more than a few reasons to love Miami, including the fact we grow the food of the gods. Really. The Latin name is Theobroma cacao. We know it as cacao or chocolate, and it grows in the tropics. Miami has a few artisanal bean-to-bar chocolatiers who source locally, and Fairchild Garden, our award-winning botanical garden, not only boasts some cacao trees, it hosts an annual Chocolate Festival. In Miami, chocolate can be local food. Yeah, we feel pretty good about that.

Cacao is fruit botanically speaking, with golden, garnet, or tawny oblong pods that grow right from the trunk. Inside is pale, sweet, sticky flesh that hugs its precious seeds. Cacao seeds are precious to humans, too. Separating the seeds—sometimes we call them cocoa beans—from the rest of the fruit takes labor. The good news is cacao's flesh, husk, and seed shells can be sustainably repurposed for uses from fuel to wellness drinks. Good thing, because we hate food waste but we love chocolate.

To get there, the cacao seeds must be fermented, toasted, then ground. This gives you a win-win—cacao nibs, the essence of chocolate, plus cacao butter, cacao's natural fat. Combine cacao nibs, cacao butter, and a little sugar—or a lot—and you've got that rich, sultry flavor and luscious mouthfeel we love.

Miami Favorites—Chocolate, Orange, and Almond Olive Oil Cake

Olive oil cakes sing of the Mediterranean. Or California. You know—places where olives grow. Florida isn't the most obvious choice, but surprise, we grow olives and press olive oil up in the panhandle near the Georgia border, where the weather's more temperate, less tropical. What we do grow in South Florida—cacao.

Whether your olive oil is from Tuscany or Tallahassee, choose a mild-tasting one here. Thanks to Fran Costigan, genius vegan pastry chef, who paved the way for fancy plant-based cakes and desserts of every stripe and flavor. This recipe is an adaptation of one of her classics.

How to serve: No sky-high layers paved with funfetti rainbow sprinkles, this cake may look plainish, but one taste commands attention. It's velvety and moist from the olive oil with a nuance of orange—chocolate plus a little Florida sunshine.

Finish with a dusting of powdered sugar, shaved dark chocolate, and/or toasted crushed almonds.

For more intense chocolate delivery, drizzle with chocolate orange glaze (p. 170).

Ingredients

- 1/2 cup unbleached all-purpose flour
- 1/4 cup whole wheat flour
- 1/4 cup Dutch process cocoa
- 1/4 cup almond flour
- 1 tablespoon cornstarch
- 1 teaspoon baking soda
- 1/4 teaspoon aluminum-free baking powder
- 3/4 cup evaporated cane sugar
- grated zest of 1 to 2 oranges (about 1 tablespoon)
- 1/2 cup fresh orange juice
- 1/2 cup plain unsweetened vegan yogurt
- 1 tablespoon cider vinegar
- 1 teaspoon almond extract or amaretto
- 1 teaspoon Grand Marnier or other orange liqueur*
- 1/3 cup olive oil

---

* Add another 2 teaspoons of fresh orange juice should you wish to skip the almond and orange liqueurs.

Instructions

- Set oven rack in the middle of the oven. Preheat oven to 350°F.
- Lightly oil an 8-inch cake pan. Line the bottom with an 8-inch round of parchment.
- In a large bowl, sift together the all-purpose flour, whole wheat flour, almond flour, cocoa, cornstarch, baking soda, and baking powder. Whisk everything gently to aerate and combine.
- In a separate bowl, whisk together cane sugar and orange zest. This will help release the orange oils in the zest. The mixture should be like damp sand. Then add the orange juice, vegan yogurt, cider vinegar, almond extract or amaretto, orange liqueur, or extra orange juice. Mix together well.
- Pour the orange mixture into the dry ingredients and give a quick but thorough stir. Then slowly pour in the olive oil. Fold everything together so batter is glossy and uniform, with no streaks of flour. Keep a light hand, don't overbeat.
- Pour the batter into the cake pan. Give the pan a light rap on the counter to expel any bubbles.
- Bake for 45 minutes or until cake is fragrant and firm, with a tester inserted in the center
- coming up clean.
- Allow to cool completely. Run a knife around the edges, invert onto a cake plate, and unmold.
- Serves 8.

Miami Flavors—Chocolate Orange Glaze

Dark and rich, this is a glaze for grownups, and another winner adapted from vegan pastry queen (and friend) Fran Costigan. Drizzle over coconut shortbread (p. 149), chocolate orange olive oil cake (p. 167), or sunshine squares (p. 152).

Ingredients

- grated rind of 1 orange
- 1/4 cup freshly squeezed orange juice
- 3-1/2 ounces dark chocolate, finely chopped
- 2 teaspoons olive oil
- 1/4 teaspoon vanilla extract or orange liqueur, such as Grand Marnier

Instructions

- In a small saucepan, stir together orange rind, orange juice, and chopped chocolate over low, low heat.
- When the chocolate starts to melt, take the saucepan off the burner and stir just until chocolate's entirely melted and the glaze is smooth and satiny.
- Stir in the olive oil and vanilla or orange liqueur to give the glaze a gloss. Pour into a bowl and set aside to cool to room temperature. Cover and chill. Keep covered and refrigerated for up to a week, during which time the glaze will thicken.
- To use, gently reheat in a saucepan over medium heat, stirring for about 5 minutes or until it's smooth and pourable.
- Makes about 1 cup, enough to lavish on the chocolate orange olive oil cake or anything you like.

Miami Favorites—Rice Pudding—Arroz con Leche

Spanish lesson—arroz con leche means rice with milk. Lost in translation though is how rice with milk becomes greater than the sum of its parts. It's like getting a hug from someone you love. Arroz con leche is Spanish-Moorish in origin, with versions across the globe, thanks to centuries of migration. Every country's, every restaurant's, every family's is the best. This one's pretty damn good too, and it's vegan. The milk is plant-based, the sweetness comes from more milk—sweetened condensed coconut milk.

White rice, rather than brown, is the rice of choice here.

How to serve: The rice pudding will need to chill a few hours before serving in order to set properly, but can be served chilled or warm or at room temperature.

It needs no more than a sprinkle of cinnamon on top, but for a grown-up garnish, soak 1/2 cup of raisins in 1/4 cup of rum, then drain the excess rum, and add the raisins to the pudding.

Ingredients

- 1 cup short-grain white rice
- 4 cups plain unsweetened oat milk or other plant-based milk
- 1 cinnamon stick
- 1 broad strip lemon zest
- 1 teaspoon vanilla
- 1 15-ounce can sweetened condensed coconut milk
- 1/4 cup evaporated cane sugar or coconut sugar, optional

Instructions

- Pour white rice into a bowl and add cold water to cover. Soak white rice for 15 minutes. Rinse rice in a strainer well so the water runs clear, not cloudy. Drain and set aside.
- In a large saucepan, heat plant-based milk over medium-high heat. Drop in the lemon zest and cinnamon stick. When it comes to a simmer, add the rice, then cook for about 20 minutes, stirring occasionally.
- Just about the time you've had it with stirring, the rice will start drinking up the plant-based milk. The mixture will thicken and smell really good—cinnamon-y, rich, and oddly sweet considering you've added no sugar.
- So add the sweetness. Pour in the sweetened condensed coconut milk, stir well to combine, and taste. It is now absolutely sweet enough for me, but if it's still a little sugar-shy for you, pour in the 1/4 cup cane or coconut sugar. Stir to dissolve. Add the vanilla.
- Keep stirring for another 15 minutes as the pudding thickens to prevent sticking or burning. If it starts to bubble, reduce heat to medium low but keep stirring until the rice yields graciously to the tooth but isn't mush.

- Remove from heat, fish out the lemon zest and cinnamon stick, and allow the pudding to cool for 30 minutes. Then cover with a lid or plastic wrap to avoid a tough pudding skin from forming and refrigerate for several hours or up to 2 days before serving. The rice pudding will continue to thicken as it cools.
- Serves 6 to 8.

Miami Flavors—Latino-Caribbean Sweet Potato Pumpkin Pie—Cazuela in a Crust

This recipe has a long name and a longer backstory. Cazuela can mean baking dish or a whatever-vegetables-you've-got-to-work-with Chilean stew or, in this case, a Puerto Rican custard that marries together sweet potato and pumpkin. For many in Miami's Black community, sweet potato pie isn't just a creamy, comforting dessert; it's its own love language and a sweet symbol of Black pride. Pumpkin pie is an American Thanksgiving classic. Put them together and you get a delicious blending of Miami's culinary influences.

How to serve: Both the filling and pie dough may be made separately a day ahead, then covered and refrigerated before baking. Pie is best served at room temperature. Enjoy as is, or take it over the top with a dollop of whipped coconut cream (p. 165) or a scoop of vegan ice cream. Serve it at family celebrations, potlucks, or any occasion that brings people together.

Ingredients

For the pie shell:

- 2 cups unbleached all-purpose flour
- pinch baking powder
- 5 tablespoons evaporated cane sugar
- 8 tablespoons (1 stick) vegan butter, chilled
- 1 tablespoon aquafaba
- 1 tablespoon ice water
- 1/2 teaspoon vanilla

For the filling:

- 1/2 cup raisins
- 2 tablespoons rum, preferably a dark or spiced rum
- 1 cup sweet potato, peeled and cooked until soft or 1 cup frozen sweet potato purée, thawed
- 1 cup pumpkin purée or half a 15-ounce can pumpkin purée—plain pumpkin, not pumpkin pie filling
- 1 cup full-fat coconut milk
- 1/2 cup brown sugar
- 1 teaspoon cinnamon
- 1 teaspoon ginger

- 1/2 teaspoon nutmeg
- 1/2 teaspoon clove
- 2 tablespoons aquafaba
- 3 tablespoons cornstarch

Instructions

For the pie shell:

- Pulse flour, baking powder, and sugar in a food processor. Add vegan butter and pulse until coarse. Add aquafaba, ice water, and vanilla. Pulse again until the consistency of damp sand. The dough will not come together at this point but will still be grainy.
- Gather everything up in plastic wrap. Wrap well and refrigerate for at least an hour or overnight.
- Preheat oven to 375°F.
- Pat dough into a 9-inch tart ring or pie shell. Press the dough down firmly and prick a few times with a fork. The recipe yields more than enough for a pie, leaving you extra for decorations, if desired.
- Bake pie shell for 12–15 minutes until the crust is pale gold, and the bottom seems set. Remove from oven and let it cool slightly.

For the pie filling:

- Reduce heat to 350°F.
- Pour raisins into a small bowl. Add the rum and let the raisins macerate.
- In a food processor, whiz together the sweet potato, pumpkin, and coconut milk, until smooth and velvety.
- Pour in brown sugar, cinnamon, ginger, nutmeg, and clove, and pulse to combine. Then add the aquafaba and cornstarch and blend to combine.
- Place the partly baked tart shell on a rimmed baking sheet. Drain the excess rum from the raisins and scatter them on the bottom of the pie shell. Then pour on the sweet potato, pumpkin, and coconut milk filling, smoothing the top with the back of a spoon.
- Bake for 30 minutes or until the top is set and the center jiggles just a little. The pie will thicken and firm up as it cools.
- Serves 8.

Miami Flavors—Orange Blossom Tart for Julia Tuttle

Miami is a city built on solid limestone. It's also built on legend. Legend's a little iffier. But it tends to have something limestone lacks—romance. This recipe honors the legend of Miami, and the woman behind it, Julia Tuttle.

Julia was a transplant from Cleveland who fell for Miami hard. Back in the 1890s, she saw Miami's potential when it was little more than a flood plain with mosquitoes. The city didn't even have a train station. Palm Beach was the southernmost stop on the line. But Julia believed in Miami and she had plans. She bought up 640 acres along the Miami River, probably for dirt cheap. And as with so many Miamians after her, she was a hustler, a promoter, a developer.

Long before the days of email, Julia waged a tireless letter-writing campaign, trying to drum up investors. John D. Rockefeller turned her down. Railroad magnate Henry Flagler kept her on the hook for years. Like many a rom-com, their epistolary relationship featured delays and misunderstandings. Then nature stepped in.

While it may seem hard to believe in these days of climate change and heat advisories, it can get cold in Florida. In the winter of 1894, the temperature dipped into the teens, and much of the state suffered a hard freeze. But not Miami.

Legend has it Julia sent Flagler a box of orange blossoms fresh from her own grove. She promised him some of her land in exchange for bringing his railroad to Miami. He said yes.

Okay, it was more of a business transaction than a true romance, and we don't even know for sure if it's true. But we like this legend enough to call Julia Tuttle the Mother of Miami. This triply orange blossom tart is for her, and for you.

How to serve: Tart is best chilled and may be made several hours or even a day ahead. The whole black cardamom seeds in the crust add a haunting flavor and surprise crunch.

Ingredients

For the pastry crust:
- 1-1/4 cup unbleached all-purpose flour
- 1/4 cup evaporated cane sugar
- 1/2 teaspoon baking powder
- 1/4 cup almond flour
- 1 orange, zested
- 1 teaspoon whole cardamom seeds (not the pods)
- 7 tablespoons vegan butter
- 2 tablespoons aquafaba

For the filling:
- 8 tablespoons (1 stick) vegan butter
- 1/2 cup evaporated cane sugar

- 1 cup almond flour
- 1/4 cup fresh orange juice
- 1 tablespoon orange flower water*, or additional tablespoon orange juice
- 2 tablespoons aquafaba
- 1 orange, zested

To finish:
- 1/4 cup orange marmalade
- 2 tablespoons Cointreau, Grand Marnier, or other orange liqueur, or 2 tablespoons fresh orange juice

Instructions

For the pastry:
- In a large bowl or food processor, sift together the all-purpose flour, sugar, baking powder, and almond flour. Grate the orange zest and add cardamom seeds. Pulse in the food processor or use a large spoon or clean hands to work the butter into the flour until the mixture forms coarse crumbs. Pour in the aquafaba and mix again until the dough starts to come together.
- Gather the dough into a ball and place it on a lightly floured surface. Knead lightly until the dough is smooth and uniform. Wrap the dough well and refrigerate until firm, at least an hour. May be made ahead and kept covered and refrigerated for up to 3 days.
- Preheat oven to 375°F. Have ready a 9-inch tart pan, preferably with a removable bottom.
- Flour your work surface lightly and roll out the chilled pastry into a 10-inch round.
- Transfer the dough to the tart pan, pressing the dough into place. Patch any tears and trim any overhang. Prick the bottom and sides with a fork. Line the pie shell with parchment or foil and weigh it down with dried rice, dried beans, or pie weights.
- Bake for 10 minutes; then carefully remove the parchment or foil and the rice, beans, or pie weights. Return to oven and bake blind for another 4–5 minutes or until the bottom just sets and begins to turn golden.
- Remove tart shell from oven and set aside to cool.
- Reduce heat to 350°F.

For the filling:
- In a large bowl or standing mixer, beat the vegan butter until light and creamy. Add the orange zest, sugar, and almond flour. Carefully add the orange juice, orange flower water, and aquafaba. Combine until incorporated into a mixture with the fluffy consistency of buttercream.
- Spread filling into the pie shell, smoothing the top.

---

* Available in Middle Eastern and other specialty markets and online.

- Bake for 30 minutes or until the center just starts to set, and the whole kitchen smells sweet.
- Remove from the oven and let the tart cool.
- To finish: In a small saucepan, heat together the marmalade and Cointreau or orange juice over medium heat, stirring until thick and combined. Remove from the burner and set aside to cool.
- Using a pastry brush, paint the tart with marmalade glaze to cover the surface completely.
- Refrigerate for 2 hours or longer.
- Serves 6 to 8.

Miami Favorites—Kinda Key Lime Pie

My father considered appreciating true Key lime pie to be an essential part of my childhood education. The filling should be pale yellow and dense, not green (a sure sign of food coloring) or fluffy. And it should be made with Key limes. Key limes look like marbles. They're smallish, round, very juicy, and native to the Florida Keys. That's why we call it Key lime pie.

Dad would be between scornful and skeptical that Key lime pie could be made without eggs and dairy—using tofu, no less—and still taste authentic. Until he had a bite. It's the real Key lime deal—with a smooth, sweet, yet tart filling and a crunchy graham crust.

You don't have to be a Miami native to love Key lime pie. That's why you'll find versions of it everywhere. Most people use more commonly available Persian limes. Key limes are more tart than Persian limes, which have softer, more floral notes. Either will work in this recipe. I don't think my father would mind. But the tofu must be silken, that's tofu in its softest and most jiggly.

How to serve: Frozen. Key lime pie is best made ahead and frozen. I loved it that way as a kid. Having never experienced a proper winter, I thought it must be what snow tasted like. Okay, I was wrong about that, but I'm right about freezing Key lime pie. The texture is creamy, not icy, and the flavor stays vibrant and pure. Best of all, having a great do-ahead dessert ready in the freezer makes for easy entertaining. Take the pie out of the freezer about 5 minutes before serving, and it will slice beautifully.

Fancy it up with vegan whipped cream if you're of a mind to. Dad was a purist. So am I.

Ingredients

- 16 plain graham crackers*
- 3 tablespoons evaporated cane sugar
- 8 tablespoons (1 stick) vegan butter, melted and cooled
- 12 ounces silken tofu, (3/4 of a 16-ounce package) drained
- 3/4 cup sweetened condensed coconut milk
- 1/2 cup evaporated cane sugar
- 2/3 cup lime juice
- 3 tablespoons cornstarch

Instructions

- Preheat oven to 375°F.
- Pulse graham crackers in a food processor till they form fine crumbs. You should have 2-1/2 cups.

---

* Check the ingredient list. Many brands contain honey, a vegan no-no. Bees make honey to feed their young, and most vegans prefer to leave honey to the bees. Can't find vegan graham crackers easily? Use Biscoff cookies. They're naturally vegan.

- Add sugar and melted vegan butter. Pulse again just a few times or until the butter and graham crackers blend and look like damp sand.
- Pour graham cracker crumbs into a 9-inch Pyrex or other ovenproof 9-inch pie pan. Spread the crumbs evenly. Use a flat-bottomed drinking glass to press the crumbs firmly onto the bottom and up the sides of the pan.
- Bake the pie crust for 10 minutes or until it's golden brown and smells buttery. Remove from oven and set aside to cool.
- Wash and dry the food processor bowl. Then add the silken tofu, sweetened condensed milk, cane sugar, lime juice, and cornstarch. Whizz just until the filling ingredients combine.
- Pour Key lime filling into a medium saucepan. Bring to a boil over medium heat, whisking constantly, until the pale yellow filling thickens and turns glossy, about 8–10 minutes. Turn off the heat, but leave the pot on the burner, and continue whisking for another minute.
- Pour the filling into the pie crust, and let it sit for 1 hour until totally cool. Wrap well in plastic wrap and place in the freezer for at least 4 hours or until frozen through.
- Serves 6 to 8.

Miami Vegan Menus

Setting a Tropical Table

Getting that Miami mood starts by setting a tropical table. Bring the outside in. Lay greenery on a solid white tablecloth—or directly onto the table—to create a look of lush abundance. It's also a brilliant way to hide tablecloth spots (talking to you, Thanksgiving cranberry sauce debacle). Miami greenery is big and bold—feathery palm fronds, broad banana leaves, and the aptly named monstera. Just one can cover a table. Dried or paper versions are available online.

Want bolder or funkier? Choose batik, kantha, or tropical print table linens.

Want simpler? Bypass tablecloths entirely with placemats made with natural sustainable materials like seagrass, straw, or rattan.

Miami does not have delicate spring flowers. We go big and bright with flame-colored ginger, hibiscus in scarlet, blush and sunshine hues, show-offy orchids, and bougainvillea in hot pink, purple, and red—watch for thorns among those pretty papery blossoms. Just a few orchids or a spray of bougainvillea make a statement, but don't let it upstage your gorgeous meal.

Small.bowls of oranges, limes, or lemons invite freshness, and unlike cut flowers, they won't wilt. Pineapples, an age-old symbol of welcome and hospitality, make natural centerpieces.

White and blue plates evoke the sea even when you're inland and miles away from the water. Or go natural with coconut shells. They've been used to holding food and drink for centuries.

Add some warmth and glow with candles—votives or tea lights in colored or clear glass or in tapers in tall glass hurricane chimneys—no hurricane required (or wanted).

Etsy www.etsy.com
Lilly Pulitzer www.lillypulitzer.com

Miami Vegan Menu

Girly Brunch/Baby Shower/Mother's Day

- Vegan Cheese Scones — 6
- Dutch Baby — 5
- Seven Seed Quinoa with Spinach and Sesame — 52
- Orange-Scented Almond Cookies — 154
- Coconut Shortbread — 170
- Magic Mango Mousse — 150

Cocktail Party on the Patio

- Three Fish-Free Ceviches — 63
- Smoked Sea Dip — 29
- Pimento Cheese — 30
- Caribbean Curried Pumpkin Dip (Pumpkin Talkari) — 27
- Papaya Chutney — 120
- Hoecakes — 32
- Crudites and Flatbreads
- Magic Dust Tropical Fruit Plate — 40
- Coconut Shortbread — 149
- Sunshine Squares with Chocolate Chunks — 152
- Orange-Scented Almond Cookies — 154

Game Day Grub

- Smoked Sea Dip — 29
- Crackers and Carrot Sticks

- Collard Tacos with Chile-Charred Onion and Sweet Potato — 106
- Picadillo — 80
- Cornbread — 34
- Sunshine Squares with Chocolate Chunks — 152

Holiday Open House

- Three Fish-Free Ceviches — 63
- Paella — 96
- Caribbean Curry — 112
- Feijoada — 85
- Rice — 171
- Collard Confetti — 57
- Coconut Green Beans — 140
- Triple Gingerbread — 156
- Coconut Shortbread — 149

Valentine's Day or Anytime Romantic Dinner

- Miami Beet Salad — 56
- Fideos — 95
- Iced Cafecito — 147
- Coconut Shortbread — 149

Birthday Party for Kids

- Pimento Cheese — 30
- Breadsticks and Carrot Sticks

- Vegan Mac and Cheese — 116
- Tropical Slaw — 58
- Black Bean and Mango Salad — 45
- Ripe Sweet Plantains (Platanos Maduros) — 143
- Roasted Potatoes (Papas Asada) — 125
- Triple Gingerbread — 156
- Sunshine Squares with Chocolate Chunks — 152

Impress the In-laws or Close-the-Deal Dinner

- Caribbean Curried Pumpkin Dip (Pumpkin Talkari) — 27
- Flatbread
- Miami Beet Salad — 56
- Collard Parcels with Chile Pecan Rice — 109
- Eggplant Caviar — 138
- Orange Blossom Tart for Julia Tuttle — 175

Weeknight Family Dinner

- Collard Tacos with Chile-Charred Onion and Sweet Potato — 106
- Tacu Tacu — 90
- Rice Pudding — 171

305 Day

- Miami gets its own day on March 5—the fifth day of the third month, get it? It's for real and it's so Miami.
- Cafecito — 147
- Guava Cream Cheese Pastries — 22
- Cuban Rice and Jackfruit or Tempeh (Arroz con jaca o soya) — 78
- Ripe Sweet Plantains (Platanos Maduros) — 143
- Coconut Green Beans — 140
- Kinda Key Lime Pie — 178

Hurricane Hunker or the Menu I Hope You Never Have to Make

Due to climate change the increasing severity and unpredictability of hurricanes means being prepared for a season's worth of rain in a few hours, winds screaming at over a hundred miles per hour, devastating storm surges, tornadoes, and flash floods. Enduring such an onslaught is terrifying, but the aftermath, while not as dramatic, is a long, soul-sapping slog—weeks, even months without electricity and comfort. But oddly, you still need to eat. It's the damnedest thing. Actually, it's a wonderful thing. Appetite is your life force exerting itself even when life sucks. So here's some recipes to get you through.

Ahead of the storm make: Tropical Granola (p. 14)—It's nutrient dense with oats, dried fruit, and nuts, and keeps tightly covered.

Munch on it whenever you need.

Seven Seed Quinoa with Spinach and Sesame (p. 52)—Fresh produce, especially delicate greens likes spinach won't last long without refrigeration, so enjoy this protein-rich and satisfying salad while you can. Leftovers will even keep covered for a day without refrigeration.

Orange-Scented Almond Cookies (p. 154)—They won't make everything better but they'll help, and they keep in an airtight tin without refrigeration.

When the electricity goes, nourish yourself with these no-cook recipes:

- Fireworks Black Bean and Mango Salad — 45
- Hearts of Palm Ceviche with Grapefruit and Avocado — 66
- Cowboy Caviar — 136
- Collard Confetti — 57
- Magic Dust Tropical Fruit Plate—the spice and sweetness sparks appetite and lifts sagging spirits — 40

Acknowledgments

With gobs of gratitude to James Beard Award-winning cookbook author, friend, and badass Anna Thomas who told me to write another book, and to Tracey Broussard, friend, master mixologist, black belt, and sprinkler of magic dust who was with me the whole bumpy ride and whose guidance made this book and my life better.

To Casey Bearsch, Leigh Scott, and Crystal Murray—the mighty LCIX team. Thank you for believing in *Miami Vegan* and for your energy in bringing it to life.

Thanks to Kathleen Ballard Photography for bringing Miami's lush tropic appeal to the page.

Thank you to my loyal tribe of Broccoli Rising subscribers for reading, sharing, and tasting.

To Books and Books, Miami's stellar indie bookstore and community hub and for being a safe space in the face of censorship.

To the aptly named librarian Ellen Book and Miami Dade Public Library for being a community resource far beyond books and for giving me a platform to teach people the pleasure of plants.

To Miami International Book Fair for bringing authors and readers together.

To *VegNews, Edible South Florida, HuffPo*, and the Professor series. Writing for you makes me happy.

To Miami's local growers. Your hard work keeps us fed and grateful.

To the Greater Miami Convention and Visitors Bureau, the Florida Department of Agriculture and Consumer Services, the University of Florida Institute of Food and Agricultural Sciences, and Fairchild Tropical Garden for expertise.

To all the chefs, cookbook authors, and vegan artisans who inspire me, including José Andrés, Fran Costigan, Nina Curtis, Jeremy Ford, Sandra Gutierrez, Katie Jones of Catalyst Creamery, Carolina Molea of L'Artisane Bakery, Hettie Lui McKinnon, Joan Nathan, Andrea Nguyen, Yotam Ottolenghi, Niven Patel, Jacques Pepin, Giorgio Rapicavoli, Miyoko Schinner, Michael Schwartz, Nigel Slater, Jeremy Tower, and Paula Wolfert.

To Margot Livesey, John Dufresne, Matt Haig, Mayukh Sen, and all the authors whose writing and friendship keep me going.

To Les Dames d'Escoffier for staunch sisterhood and support.

To LDEI Grande Dame and even grander friend Bev Shaffer and grand artist and friend Laura Crabtree Hollenbeck.

To Rancho Gordo and the Beans is How Coalition. Beans are my love language.

To the Organic Marketing Association for making it fun to cheer on the good guys.

And to Miami.

About the Author

Ellen Kanner is the author of the award-winning book *Feeding the Hungry Ghost: Life, Faith and What to Eat for Dinner*. She writes about the intersection of food, culture, community, wellness, and sustainability for outlets including *HuffPo, VegNews,* and *Edible South Florida,* which calls her "the lovable and entertaining voice of plant-based." She's a vegan advocate and culinary instructor, recipe developer for major brands, and the creator of the Substack newsletter Broccoli Rising. A fifth-generation Miami native, she lives with her husband in—where else?—Miami.

Index

A

ackee, 10
agave, 58, 139
aji amarillo paste, 90
alfalfa sprouts, 56
all-purpose flour, 176
allspice, 19, 69, 120, 136–138, 156
all-star upside down cake, 159–160
almonds, 28, 55, 58
    chocolate, orange, and almond olive oil
        cake, 167–168
    flour, 19, 154, 162, 167–168, 175–176
    milk, 162
    orange blossom tart, 175–177
    orange-scented almond cookies,
        154–155
    pumpkin bread, 28
    strawberry kuchen, 162
amaretto, 167–168
amchoor or sumac, 39
ancho chile, 96
angel hair pasta, 98–99
angel hair with pumpkin, annatto, and lime,
    98–100
annatto, 86, 98, 101
anytime romantic dinner, 184
apple cider vinegar, 30, 86, 88, 118, 122,
    167–168
apricot jam, 124
aquafaba, 5, 12, 19, 28, 34, 147, 150, 152, 154,
    173–176
arroz con jaca o soya, 78–79, 184
arroz con leche, 171–172
artichoke, 29
arugula, 42, 45, 48–50, 56
avocado, 50, 60–61, 63, 66, 105

B

baguette, 12
Bahamian chowder, 69–71
baking powder, 5–6, 8, 17, 28, 34, 159, 161–162,
    167–168, 173–176
baking soda, 17, 28, 156, 167
bananas, 40
    French toast with caramelized, 12–13
    tropical porridge, 15
basil, 130
bay leaf, 70, 78, 85
beans, 50, 81–82, 84, 90
bean sprouts, 61
beetroots, 56
beet sprouts, 56
berries, 15, 159, 162–163
birthday party for kids menu, 184
biscuits
    cat head, 8–9
bittersweet chocolate, 152
black beans, 85, 88, 136–137
black-eyed peas, 136–137
Black Girl Baking (Jerrelle Guy), 162
black rice, 73, 108
blueberry loaf, 17–18
Bomba rice, 96–97
bread
    coconut shortbread, 149, 183
    cornbread, 34–35, 69, 184
    flatbreads, 183–184
    gingerbread, triple, 156–157, 184
    mango quick bread, 19–20
    persimmon, 19
    pumpkin, 28
brown rice, 73, 78–79, 90, 108
brown sugar, 12, 152, 159, 162,
    173–174

C

cabbage, 46, 54, 58, 60, 112, 122
cacao, 166
cacao butter, 166
cacao nibs, 166
Cafecito culture, 2–3, 147
café con leche, 2–3
caffeine-free espresso powder, 147
calabaza, 101, 112
calabaza stars, 26
callaloo, 54
Calle Ocho cafes, 2

cane sugar, 4, 17, 19, 46, 60–61, 136–137, 143, 147, 149, 152, 156, 159, 161, 163, 167–168, 171, 173, 175, 178–179
capers, 79–80
cardamom seeds, 175
Caribbean curried pumpkin dip (pumpkin talkari), 26–27, 183–184
Caribbean curry, 85, 112–114, 184
Caribbean pigeon peas and rice, 58, 92–93
carrots, 58, 60, 69, 112, 122
    carrot sticks, 183
    carrot tops, 54
cashew cream, 132
cashews, 14, 30, 40, 50, 113, 120
Catalan spinach, 55, 81, 94
cat head biscuits, 8–9
cauliflower, 50, 112
cayenne, 30, 143
Cazuela, 173–174
celery, 45, 69, 75
ceviche, 62, 66
chaat masala, 38–39
chard, 54
cherry tomatoes, 49
chickpeas, 81, 94–95
    flour, 5, 49, 140
    with saffron, 81–83
    tofu, 49–50
chile powder, 39, 105–106
chimichurri, 123
chocolate, orange, and almond olive oil cake, 167–169
chocolate orange glaze, 170
choka, 47
cider vinegar, 6, 8
cilantro leaves, 45–46, 49, 58, 61, 63, 65–66, 81–82, 98, 101, 105, 108, 113, 120, 123, 128, 136, 140
cinnamon, 19, 26, 28, 152, 156, 171, 173–174
clove, 55, 156, 174
clover sprouts, 56
cobblers, 161
cocktail party menu, 183
cocoa beans, 166
coconut green beans, 140–141, 184
coconut milk, 12, 68, 111–113, 165, 173–174
    sweetened condensed, 150, 171, 178
coconut oil, 49, 112, 120, 128, 140, 149

coconut shortbread, 149, 183
coconut sugar, 46, 58, 143, 171
coffee, 2, 156
    Cafecito culture, 2–3, 147
    Cuban, 4, 147
    iced cafecito, 147–148
colada, 3
cole slaw, 58–59
collard greens, 54, 57, 104, 106, 108–109, 128, 139
    collard confetti, 57, 85, 90, 184–185
    collard parcels with Chile pecan rice, 108–110, 184
    collard tacos with chile-charred onion and sweet potato, 105–107, 184
Common Threads, p. 128
coriander, 108, 112–113, 128
corn, 101, 130, 136–137
cornbread, 34–35, 69, 184
cornmeal, 32, 132
    mush grits, 132
cornstarch, 167–168, 174, 178
Costigan, Fran, 167, 170
cowboy caviar, 136–137, 185
crackers, 183
cream of tartar, 147, 150, 154
cremini, 65
Creole or blackened seasoning, 75
crispy grits cakes, 134–135
crudites, 183
crystallized ginger, 40
Cuban black beans, 85, 88–89
Cuban coffee (café Cubano), 4, 147
Cuban rice and jackfruit or tempeh, 78–79, 184
cucumber, 60
cumin, 39, 45, 49, 52, 78–80, 85, 98, 112–113, 128, 136–137, 140
cumin seed, 26, 105
6-cup moka pot, 2, 4
curry/curries, 111
curry leaves, 26, 111–112, 140
curry powder, 111

D

dandelion greens, 54
dark chocolate, 147
demerara sugar, 149
djon djon rice, 73–74

Dutch baby, 5, 183
Dutch process cocoa, 167

E

eggplant, 47, 50, 140, 163
    eggplant caviar, 138, 184
escarole, 54
espresso powder, 2–4, 147
Étouffée, 75
evaporated cane sugar, 19

F

feijoada, 85–87, 184
fennel bulb, 69
fennel seed, 26, 52, 94
fideuà (fideos), 94–95
fireworks black bean and mango salad, 45, 185
Flagler, Henry, 175
flatbreads, 183–184
French toast with caramelized bananas, 12–13

G

game day grub menu, 183–184
garam masala, 49, 112
garlic, 46, 49, 52, 57, 68–69, 73, 75, 78, 80–81, 85–86, 90, 94, 98–99, 101, 105, 108, 112, 118, 120, 122–123, 125, 128, 138
    powder, 30, 43, 78–79, 126
ginger, 19, 28, 46, 49, 60, 112–113, 120, 128, 140, 156, 173–174
gingerbread, triple, 156–157, 184
girly brunch/baby shower/mother's day menu, 183
graham crackers, 178
Grand Marnier, 152, 154, 167, 170, 176
granola, tropical, 14, 185
grapefruit, 40, 66
grapes, 40, 49, 62, 158
    hearts of palm ceviche with grapefruit and avocado, 66, 185
grapeseed oil, 17, 19, 112, 120, 128, 140, 156
grape tomatoes, 5, 42–43, 48, 63, 98, 130, 136
Gratitude Gardens, p. 72
green beans, 140–141
green mango salad, 46
green olives, 79–80
green pepper, 65, 130
green plantain, 101–102, 112
greens, 54
green salad, 81, 88, 92, 94, 108, 115, 124, 130, 158
guava, 21–22
    cream cheese pastry, 22–23, 184

H

Haitian bean gravy, 68, 128
Hearst, William Randolph, 77
hearts of palm, 60–61
    ceviche with grapefruit and avocado, 66, 185
Hemings, James, 115
hemp seeds, 52
hing (asafoetida), 140
hoecakes, 32–33, 183
holiday open house menu, 184
Hopkins House, p. 125
Hurston, Zora Neale, 118

I

iced cafecito, 147–149, 184
impress the in-laws or close-the-deal dinner menu, 184
Indian dal curry, 111

J

jackfruits, 78–79, 139
    Cuban rice and jackfruit or tempeh, 78–79, 184
jalapeño pepper, 10, 45, 49, 65–66, 69, 73, 75, 86, 88, 105, 108–109, 112, 118, 120, 123, 130, 136–138
Jamaican curry powder, 26, 58, 112
Jefferson, Thomas, 115
jicama, 46, 58, 61, 63

K

Kahlua, 147
kale, 54, 88, 128, 130
Kinda Key lime pie, 178–180, 184
kuchen, 162
kumquats, 56

L

Latin and Caribbean communities, in Miami, 77, 84

Latino-Caribbean sweet potato pumpkin pie, 173–174
lemon, 15, 30, 57
    juice, 15, 29–30, 40, 42–43, 57, 63, 123, 128, 138, 156
    zest, 171–172
lemongrass, 46
lentils, brown, 80
lettuce leaves, 54, 61
    lettuce cups, 61
lime juice, 26, 38, 40, 45–46, 48–49, 58, 63, 65, 98–99, 108, 113, 120, 122, 136–137, 143, 150, 178
liquid aminos, 118

M

Madison, Deborah, 19
magic dust, 38–39
    tropical fruit plate, 40–41, 183, 185
magic mango mousse, 149–151, 183
maitake mushroom, 75
mamaliga, 132
mangoes, 40, 45
    mango barbecue sauce, 118
    mango purée, 118, 150
    mango quick bread, 19–20
maque choux, 130–131
mayonnaise, vegan, 29–30, 42
Miami beet salad, 56, 184
Miami vegan lettuce cups with heart, 60–61
Miami vegan menu, 183–184
microgreens, 40, 54
mint leaves, 40, 46, 61, 120
miso, 30, 101, 139
molasses, 28, 118, 156
Momma's greens-Sukuma Wiki, 128–129
Monastery Church of Saint Bernard de Clairvaux, 77
mushrooms, 5, 72
    djon djon rice, 73–74
    mushroom ceviche, 65
    mushroom Étouffée, 75–76
mustard greens, 54
mustard seeds, 112, 120

N

Napa cabbage, 58
nectarines, 40
nigella (black onion seeds), 26
no-cook recipes, 185
ñora, 96–97
nori dust, 29, 69–70, 121
nori sheet, 65, 94, 96–97, 121
nutmeg, 19, 28, 156, 174
nutritional yeast, 5–6, 10, 30, 108, 115, 125

O

oat milk, unsweetened, 6, 8, 12, 19, 34, 108, 115, 161, 171
Old Bay seasoning, 70
olive oil, 5, 10, 32, 43, 47–49, 52, 55–57, 68–69, 73, 78, 80, 85, 90–91, 94–95, 97–98, 101, 105–106, 108, 118, 123–124, 126, 130, 136–138, 167, 170
onion powder, 78–79
onions, 10, 63, 65–66, 68–69, 73, 75, 78, 80–81, 85–86, 90, 94, 98, 101, 105, 108, 112, 118, 122, 125, 128, 136–138
orange pepper, 65, 101, 130
oranges, 40, 85–86, 152, 154, 167, 170
    blossom tart, 175–177, 184
    juice, 17, 52, 56, 60, 63, 122, 124, 152, 163, 167–168, 170, 176
    liqueur, 152, 154, 167–168, 170, 176
    marmalade, 176–177
    orange-scented almond cookies, 154–155, 183, 185
    zest, 175–176
oregano, 78–80, 85, 90
overnight oats, 15

P

paella, 96–97, 184
palm sugar, 60
panzanella, 42–44
papaya, 40, 63, 116, 119
    chutney, 120, 183
    face mask, 119
    tofu ceviche, 63–64
paprika, 30, 80–81, 94, 126
Paradise Farms, p. 72
parsley, 63, 123, 138
pasta, 115
pastelitos de guayaba, 21–23, 184

peaches, 40
peach jam, 124
peanuts, 46, 113
pears, 40
peas, 79, 94–95
pecans, 108
persimmon bread, 19
picadillo, 80, 184
pie shell and pie filling, 174
pigeon peas, 136–137
pikliz, 122
pimentos, 79
    cheese, vegan, 8, 30–31, 183–184
pineapple, 40, 112–113
pine nuts, 55, 138
pistachios, 40, 55
plantains, 142
plant-based milk, 5, 14–15, 19, 34, 115, 156, 162, 171. *see also* coconut milk; oat milk, unsweetened
platanos maduros, 143–144, 184
plums, 40
polenta, 132
pomegranate seeds, 52, 56
Ponce de Leon, 77, 136
porridge, tropical, 15–16
potatoes, 69–70, 112
    roasted potatoes-papas asada, 126–127, 184
powdered sugar, 12, 22, 152, 154, 156, 162, 165, 167
puddings, 163–164
puff pastry, 21–23
pulse flour, 174
pumpkin, 24–25, 99, 174
    bread, 28
    cubes, 24
    facial mask, 25
    pie, 173–174
    purée, 24–26
    seeds, 14, 45, 52, 105
    Seminole, 24
    steaming, 25

Q

quinoa, 52
    seven seed quinoa with spinach and sesame dressing, 52–53, 183, 185

R

radish, 50, 54, 63, 105
raisins, 19, 28, 55, 173–174
red beans, 68
red pepper, 10, 45, 58, 60, 63, 65, 69, 78, 86, 88, 122, 125, 130, 136–137
red rice, 108
red wine, 75–76, 94–95
red wine vinegar, 123, 136–137
refried beans, 105
remoulade sauce, 42
rice, 84, 184
    pudding, 171–172, 184
roasted potatoes-papas asada, 126–127, 184
Rockefeller, John D, 175
rolled oats, 14–15
rum, 147, 150, 159

S

saffron, 81, 94, 98
sancocho, 85, 101–103
sandwich filling, 29
scallions, 10, 61, 68, 136
Scotch bonnet pepper, 49, 63, 122
Seed Food and Wine, p. 52
Seminole pumpkin, 24
sesame oil, 60
sesame seeds, 52, 60.
    see also tahini dressing
seven seed quinoa with spinach and sesame dressing, 52–53, 183, 185
sherry vinegar, 55–56, 88
shiro miso, 139
Shulman, Martha Rose, 19
Silpats, 43, 50
smoked fish dip, 29, 183
smoked paprika, 86, 88, 90, 118, 130, 139
smoked sea dip, 29
sofkee, 132–134
sofrito, 47, 81–82, 86
SOL Mushrooms, p. 72
Sos pwa, 68
soy sauce, 46, 60, 118
spaghetti, 98
spinach, 5, 42, 45, 49, 55, 124, 130
    Catalan spinach, 55, 81, 94

  Miami beet salad, 56
  seven seed quinoa with spinach and sesame dressing, 52–53, 183, 185
sprouts, 26, 50, 56, 61, 78
starfruit (carambola), 15, 158–159
steel cut oats (pinhead oats), 15
strawberries, 40
  strawberry kuchen, 162
  strawberry pudding, 163–164
styrofoam cup, 3
sugar, 2–3, 14, 21, 28, 34, 146, 166, 176. *see also* cane sugar; coconut sugar
  industry, 146
  palm, 60
  powdered, 22, 154, 156, 165, 167
summer fruit cobbler, 161
summer squash casserole, 125
sunflower seeds, 14, 30, 52
sunflower shoots, 56
sunshine squares with chocolate chunks, 152–153, 183–184
swamp cabbage, 66
sweetened condensed coconut milk, 150, 171, 178
sweet potato, 101, 106, 173
sweet potatoes, 105
sweet potato pumpkin pie, Latino-Caribbean, 173–174
Swiss chard, 88

T

tacu tacu, 90–92, 184
tadka, 26
tahini dressing, 49, 52, 56
Tajin spice, 38–39
tamari, 60, 118
tamarind, 140
  vinaigrette, 92, 108, 124, 130
tangerine, 56
tempeh, 29
  Cuban rice and jackfruit or tempeh, 78–79, 184
  house-smoked, 90, 118, 139
Thai basil, 61
Thai red curry, 111
three fish-free ceviches, 183–184
305 day menu, 184
thyme, 73, 75, 126, 130

thyme leaves, 68–69
toasted breadcrumbs, 115
toasted cornbread croutons, 42
tofu, 5, 61, 70, 178
tofu scramble, 10–11
tomato choka, 48
  salad with chickpea tofu, 49–51
tomatoes, 63, 65, 69, 75, 78, 80–81, 94, 98, 105, 128, 130, 136–138
  paste, 69–70, 86, 88, 94–95, 101–102, 112–113, 138
  purée, 118
toppings/garnishings
  Caribbean curried pumpkin dip (pumpkin talkari), 26
  chickpeas with saffron, 82
  collard tacos with chile-charred onion and sweet potato, 106
  Dutch baby, 5
  eggplant caviar, 138
  for feijoada, 85
  Fireworks Black Bean and Mango Salad, 45
  French toast with caramelized bananas, 12
  magic dust tropical fruit plate, 40
  magic mango mousse, 150
  Miami vegan lettuce cups with heart, 60
  papaya-tofu ceviche, 63
  rice pudding, 171
  seven seed quinoa with spinach and sesame dressing, 53
  Sos pwa, 68
  strawberry kuchen, 162
  tomato choka salad with chickpea tofu, 49
  vegan cheese scones, 6–7
tortillas, 105–106
tostones, 142
Trini choka, 47
triple gingerbread, 156–157, 184
tropical fruit plate with magic dust, 40–41
tropical table, setting, 183
turmeric, 30, 52, 78–79, 112–113, 120, 128, 140
turnip greens, 54, 130
Tuttle, Julia, 175–177, 184

U

unbleached all-purpose flour, 5–6, 17, 19, 28, 149, 152, 156, 159, 161–162, 167, 173, 175

unsweetened applesauce, 152, 156, 159–160
unsweetened coconut flakes, 14–15, 140

V

Valentine's day dinner, 184
vanilla, 12, 19, 130, 147, 149–150, 165, 170–171, 173–174
vegan butter, 5–6, 8, 12, 28, 32, 34, 75–76, 115, 125, 132, 143, 149, 159, 161–162, 174–176, 178–179
vegan cheese scones, 6–7, 183
vegan macaroni and cheese, 115
vegan pimento cheese, 8
vegan yogurt, 5
    all-star upside down cake, 159–160
    chocolate, orange, and almond olive oil cake, 167–168
    Dutch baby, 5
    summer blueberry loaf, 17
    unsweetened, 17, 159, 167–168

vegetable broth, 75, 78, 98, 101, 105, 128
Vidalia, 136
Vitamix, 106

W

walnuts, 56, 80
weeknight family dinner, 184
wheat flour, 8, 19, 156, 167–168
whipped coconut cream, 156, 161, 165
White Lily flour, 8
white wine, 69–70, 78–79
whole wheat flour, 28, 156, 167

Y

yam, 101–102
yellow pepper, 65, 101
yellow squash, 10, 125

Z

zucchini, 10, 42, 50, 140

www.ingramcontent.com/pod-product-compliance
Lightning Source LLC
Chambersburg PA
CBHW061354010526
44107CB00011B/932